Hotel Internal Control Guide

This publication is the product of a subcommittee of the Committee on Financial Management of the American Hotel & Motel Association.

- W. Peter Temling, CPA, Chairman, Carnival Hotels & Casinos
- Susan J. Claremont, Director of Internal Audit, Marriott International, Inc.
- John E. Nichols, Director of Internal Audit, Westin Hotels & Resorts I-A
- Richard DesVaux, Vice President of Internal Audit, Hilton Hotels Corporation
- Richard Piluso, Vice President of Internal Audit, Loews Corporation
- Randy Karns, Partner, Arthur Andersen & Company

The subcommittee would like to thank A. Neal Geller in particular for his pioneering work in the area of internal control, evidenced in part by his book *Internal Control: A Fraud-Prevention Handbook for Hotel and Restaurant Managers*, published by the School of Hotel Administration at Cornell University. Professor Geller's book is available from the Cornell Campus Store. For orders and prices: Telephone, 607-255-5121; fax, 607-254-8075; e–mail, csbooks@cornell.edu.

Disclaimer

This publication is designed to provide accurate and authoritative information in regard to the subject matter covered. It is sold with the understanding that the publisher is not engaged in rendering legal, accounting, or other professional service. If legal advice or other expert assistance is required, the services of a competent professional person should be sought.

—*From the Declaration of Principles jointly adopted by the American Bar Association and a Committee of Publishers and Associations*

Nothing contained in this publication shall constitute a standard, an endorsement, or a recommendation of the Educational Institute of the American Hotel & Motel Association (the Institute) or the American Hotel & Motel Association (AH&MA). The Institute and AH&MA disclaim any liability with respect to the use of any information, procedure, or product, or reliance thereon.

©Copyright 1997
By the EDUCATIONAL INSTITUTE of the
AMERICAN HOTEL & MOTEL ASSOCIATION
1407 South Harrison Road
P.O. Box 1240
East Lansing, Michigan 48826

The Educational Institute of the
American Hotel & Motel Association
is a nonprofit educational foundation.

Printed in the United States of America
1 2 3 4 5 6 7 8 9 10 01 00 99 98 97

ISBN 0-86612-153-6

AH&MA Internal Audit Subcommittee
Hotel Internal Control Guide

Contents

Introduction

Most of this introduction is drawn verbatim from A. Neal Geller, *Internal Control: A Fraud-Prevention Handbook for Hotel and Restaurant Managers* (Ithaca, N.Y.: Cornell School of Hotel Administration, 1991).

Proposed Statement of Objectives

The objective of this guide is to summarize the internal control procedures necessary to minimize operational risks and provide assurance that management's objectives are being met.

What Is Internal Control?

To a hotel operator or manager, internal control is the aspect of management that deals with prevention of fraud and embezzlement. Internal control is an accounting function or topic, since it often deals with such items as money, records, and documents. And it is a function of the general manager and top management, because it deals with all aspects of the operation. Indeed, if a hotel is to develop and implement good internal controls, and thus be reasonably assured that it is preventing theft and embezzlement, top management must be thoroughly involved at all phases.

Here is an official accounting definition of internal control:

Internal control comprises the plan of organization and all of the coordinate methods and measures adopted within a business to safeguard its assets, check the accuracy and reliability of its accounting data, promote operational efficiency, and encourage adherence to the prescribed managerial policies. This definition is possibly broader than the meaning sometimes attributed to the term. It recognizes that a system of internal control extends beyond those matters which relate directly to the functions of the accounting and financial departments. A well-developed system of internal controls might include budgetary controls, standard costs, periodic operating reports, statistical analyses, a personal training program and an internal audit staff.[1]

From that rather long definition can be extracted four central points that divide into two groups:

- Accounting Controls
  1. Safeguard assets, and
  2. Ensure the accuracy and reliability of accounting data.
- Administrative Controls
  1. Promote operational efficiency, and
  2. Encourage adherence to management's policies.

The purpose of this book is the prevention of fraud and embezzlement, so the controls discussed here will primarily be accounting controls. Administrative controls, particularly those that ensure adherence to managerial policy, are also important for internal control and the prevention of fraud and embezzlement. They entail the set of standard operating procedures (SOPs) that ensure that controls are properly implemented and followed. Administrative controls must, however, follow well-developed accounting controls.

Conditions for Fraud and Embezzlement

Three environmental conditions are necessary for fraud or embezzlement to take place. They are:

- Need,
- Opportunity, and
- Failure of conscience.

Need refers to the economic or psychological deficiencies that drive people to steal. It is an area that unfortunately has received too much attention over the years. Hotel and restaurant operators are constantly admonished to "watch their employees' lifestyles" to assess whether they are "living beyond their means." Books on crime have dealt with the subject, even developing catchy phrases like "the three Bs" (booze, bookies, and babes): when any employee indulged in one of the "Bs," he or she required special watching.[2] Not only is the "three Bs" idea sexist and outdated, it represents foolish advice. All employees, including top management, have economic and other needs. In fact, one could argue that economic needs drive good employees to produce! Focusing on the need condition puts managerial energy in the wrong areas—areas that managers can do little about.

It is the second condition, *opportunity,* upon which management can exert some productive influence. If management can preclude the opportunity for stealing, then it can truly prevent fraud and embezzlement. The purpose of this book is to help one set up accounting functions, revenue functions, cash functions, and other asset functions in such a way that there is no opportunity for theft. Clearly, the best way to prevent theft is to eliminate the opportunity.

The third condition, *failure of conscience,* involves conditions that allow a thief to rationalize the act of stealing. People need to rationalize theft. They need to convince themselves that they are somehow justified in taking what does not belong to them. Unlike economic and psychological needs, however, management can have some indirect influence on this need. That influence comes from creating an environment where it is difficult to rationalize acts against the operation. One way to accomplish this is to apply internal control principles firmly but evenly throughout the organization, having the same rules for top management as for other employees. In this way, one precludes discriminatory feelings and grumbling on the part of the line staff. If all managers are required to sign a check for food and drink in the same manner any hotel guest would, an atmosphere of control and recordkeeping prevails. If management, on the other hand, simply picks up a soft drink or pastry in a casual manner, the atmosphere that prevails may well be one of "the boss takes what he or she wants, why shouldn't I?" Similar situations exist for such issues as steward's sales (when merchandise is sold to staff at reduced rates), searching packages at the door, and punching-in at the time clocks. The rules should be applied evenly across the board, thus precluding one important avenue of rationalization.

In summary, of the three environmental conditions necessary for fraud and embezzlement to take place, the condition upon which management can exert the most influence is opportunity. Therefore, it makes the most sense to treat precluding or preventing opportunity as the key control objective. Most of the principles of control that follow in this book have as their primary goal removing all opportunities for theft.

Hospitality Industry Characteristics

All businesses have areas of weakness and vulnerability to fraud and embezzlement. Hospitality businesses have the same general control weaknesses that affect all enterprises. In addition, the hospitality industry has the following general operating characteristics that render it relatively more vulnerable to theft:

- Many cash transactions,
- Small businesses,
- Relatively low-skill jobs,
- Positions with low social status,
- Items of relatively high value (e.g., wine), and
- The use of commodities.

Cash. Much has been said in the popular and business press of how the world is moving toward a "cash-less" society. With the widespread use of hotel charge accounts, credit cards, debit cards, and, in the near future, "smart cards," it is true that far less cash changes hands in many hotel transactions. Most hotels today require guests to present a major credit card for registration and for the establishment of credit, regardless of how the guest wishes to settle the bill. In spite of that fact, hotels still need to maintain and deal with a great deal of cash. For one thing, the guests expect it. Guests want easy access to cash for tipping, shopping, entertainment and recreation, and foreign exchange. Most hotels also have numerous revenue outlets that are open for long hours, requiring many more cashier shifts and cash banks than businesses that have a single revenue outlet operating only from nine to five.

Size. Even though many properties are large and many hotels are part of a chain, a hotel operates primarily like a small business. Even large hotels are aggregations of many relatively small revenue outlets. In a large, modern, full-service hotel, the rooms department may be a fairly large revenue center, but there will be many bars, restaurants, and other revenue centers that individually are small operations. Thus, the critical mass or economies of scale that help larger operations with efficiency and control are often lacking.

Job Status. As a service business that operates 24 hours a day, seven days per week, a hotel comprises many unskilled, low-paying jobs. Most revenue dollars are brought in by wait staff, food and beverage cashiers, and front office clerks. The high turnover and low social status that often comes with that type of employment does little to help the internal control environment. Automation is raising the skill levels necessary in many of these jobs, but it will be a long time before growth and economic viability raise the overall standard.

Commodities. The items of inventory used in the hospitality industry are commodities—that is, goods that employees would normally need and buy for their own consumption. The industry is, after all, providing lodging and food, and most people need to provide lodging and food for themselves and their families. At the same time, the inventory items are also of high value relative to their size and weight. Seafood, steak, good wine, and other items can have considerable cost and sales value, yet do not take a good deal of space and are easily concealed or consumed.

General Principles of Good Internal Control

Exhibit 1.1 lists ten general principles of internal control. These principles apply to all business enterprises.

The following pages discuss the way these factors apply in particular to the hospitality industry. In addition to these general principles, there are two mechanical processes that are important in a general way to all internal control procedures. These are the concepts of the audit trail and accounting documentation, both of which will also be discussed in this chapter.

Exhibit 1.1
General Principles of Internal Control

1. Maintain a division of duties.
2. Fix responsibility in one individual.
3. Limit the number of employees with access to assets.
4. Keep cash banks and stores to a minimum.
5. Make internal control preventative, not detective.
6. Have third-party employees perform surprise counts.
7. Bond employees with access to cash, records, or stores.
8. Schedule mandatory vacations and rotate employees.
9. Conduct frequent external audits.
10. Use cost-benefit analysis.

Maintain a Division of Duties

Division of duties, also referred to as separation of duties and segregation of duties, is the most important principle of internal control. It is also the most pervasive concept, so it will be discussed specifically in nearly every chapter of this book.

Division of duties is a simple but powerful concept. Here's how it works: No one individual should have total control over any transaction. If there are two or more people involved with each transaction, it would take collusion (i.e., a conspiracy) between those two (or more) persons in order to falsify or otherwise change that transaction. One important way to implement the principle of division of duties would be to keep the custody of assets separate from the recordkeeping or accountability for those assets. In a hotel, cash handling is kept separate from bookkeeping. Front office cashiers, for example, have constant custody of large sums of cash. Why can't they simply take a handful? Because in a well-controlled operation, they have custody of the cash, but they do not have access to or control over the accountability for that cash. Their original bank, or float, is issued by another person who records the amount and shift time of that issue. The individual banks are also recorded in the general ledger by yet another person. The transactions that change the cashier's bank during the shift—such as revenue collections—may be posted by the cashier, but are likewise not under his or her total control. As we will see in later chapters, revenue generation and recording—whether in rooms, food and beverage, or other areas—are fairly complex transactions involving several persons. So, our cashier has custody and access, but cannot control the accountability. An income auditor may have access to the audit trail and accountability, but should not have access to the cash. As transactions get more complicated, more people are involved, making collusion more difficult.

The essential preventative role that division of duties plays is that when several people are involved in a transaction (that is, no one person has complete control), collusion becomes a necessary condition to fraud or embezzlement. Collusion is a difficult and fragile process to achieve. When two or more people must collude to perpetrate a fraud, the probability of that fraud coming to fruition is far smaller than if one of the individuals had complete control.

Limitations. Division of duties, by itself, is not sufficient to prevent internal control problems. The division must be an effective one. If a hotel gives two relatives (or two lifelong friends) control over parts of a transaction, the separation may not be effective. Division of duties also can be expensive, and adding staff strictly for the sake of accomplishing it is generally not recommended. As stated in the preface, when operations are small, and effective division of duties may be difficult to cost-justify, management must assume more of the duties. If duties must be combined, moreover, such combination should involve management personnel. More discussion of that concept will appear in later chapters.

Division of duties must be combined with other principles to yield effective internal controls. In the chapters that follow, where specific internal control principles are discussed, division of duties will appear again—usually as the first item of discussion—and the specific divisions of tasks will be explained.

Fix Responsibility in One Individual

Where practical, responsibility for a given activity should always be designated to a single individual. In that way, the person can be informed of his or her responsibilities, be given a set of standard operating procedures, and be expected to adhere to them. If the responsibility is given to one individual, then management knows where to start looking when there is a problem. This principle should also be viewed from the employees' perspective, however. The employees are held responsible for assets or actions, so they need the conditions to allow them to carry out their responsibilities. For example, a front office cashier should be solely and fully responsible for his or her bank. Consequently, no one but that individual should have access to that bank. There should be no sharing of banks and no sharing of custody. It is unfair to make a person responsible for a bank and then give others access to it.

Limit the Number of Employees with Access to Assets

The more people with access to cash or merchandise inventories, the greater the risk of losses—whether by actual theft, or by simple mismanagement. This principle is common sense. The principle also fits well with the one above: fixing responsibility. Responsibility for an asset cannot be fixed in a single individual (or the smallest group) if there is unlimited access to the asset. Limiting access, however, has some operational trade-offs.

Keep Cash Banks and Stores to a Minimum

The principle of keeping cash banks and stores, or inventories, to a minimum improves control in much the same way as limited access does: it lowers the risk. It also has the advantage of fitting very well with the modern management tools of cash management and inventory management. Those concepts help lower costs and increase profits by the scientific management of cash and other assets.[3]

Minimizing cash banks and stores and limiting access to them, however, will force management to make operational trade-offs called "control/policy trade-offs," a term used throughout the book and a recurring problem in the field of internal control. A conflict or trade-off often exists between good internal controls and operating policy—especially operating policy that is geared toward good guest service and ease of operation. While limiting access and minimizing stores provide better control, those procedures may make it more difficult or complicated to provide excellent and fast service. For example, a hotel is more likely to run out of a guest's favorite brandy if it minimizes stock. And then it will compound the problem by requiring several signatures, including that of the general manager, to gain entry to the liquor storeroom for another bottle! Similarly, minimizing the size of cash banks makes sense from a control perspective, but the hotel's image may suffer if a clerk needs to tell a guest that he or she does not currently have enough cash in the drawer to change a $100 bill!

Thus, a trade-off often exists between ideal control and the policies of management that may have as objectives good or fast service, good employee relations, or simple cost savings. Such trade-offs will be encountered frequently in this book, and they will be discussed as they arise. The general rule, however, is to strive for the most ideal control and then have management modify the control procedures as necessary. Management must always be aware, however, of the increased control risks involved in stepping away from ideal controls.

Make Internal Control Preventative, Not Detective

The nature of internal control and the fact that it deals with fraud and embezzlement—crimes for sure—lead a lot of managers to want to play detective. After all, if you are concerned that your employees are stealing from you, you want to catch the thieves! There is nothing wrong with a wish to ferret out and punish thieves. A far more effective program, however, is one that prevents the thefts in the first place. Remember that the primary objective of an internal control program is to preclude the opportunity for theft. That is prevention, and in the long run, it is far more productive and cost effective than detection. In fact, with the proper prevention, there will be nothing to detect! Throughout the balance of the book, prevention will be the primary focus. However, it will become apparent that this emphasis can also cause some conflicts.

Have Third-Party Employees Perform Surprise Counts

Surprise counts of cashier shifts, merchandise, storeroom inventories, and bars should be performed frequently enough so that they become expected. The word "surprise" refers to the exact timing and location of the counts. They are random, but not unexpected. In fact, if the counts were truly unexpected, they would be in direct conflict with the principle that internal control should be preventative, not detective. The fact that surprise counts are made frequently and are written up in job descriptions and standard operating procedures (SOPs) is what turns a normally detective endeavor into a preventative one. Cash-handling, inventory-handling, and accounting employees should expect surprise counts or shutdowns of their shifts on a random basis. Obviously, if such counts were made systematically, they would be useless. For example, if you count the cash bank in the rooftop bar every fourth Thursday of the month precisely at 4:00 PM, you can almost guarantee that it will be fine! The random counts should be performed by third-party employees who do not normally count that cash or take that inventory. It is a good idea, for instance, for top management to get involved occasionally with this important part of the internal control program.

Bond Employees with Access to Cash, Records, or Stores

All accounting, cash-handling, inventory-handling, and top-management employees should be bonded through an insurance policy called a "fidelity bond." A fidelity bond is a type of insurance that protects the hotel against losses from employee dishonesty. As with fire insurance, when the hotel experiences a loss, the bonding company reimburses it for the amount of the loss (up to the limits of the policy). In fidelity bonding, the losses are those related to employee dishonesty.

In addition to loss recovery, fidelity bonding is a strong deterrent to fraud and embezzlement by employees. That aspect, other characteristics of fidelity bonding, and the legal environment in general are discussed in greater detail in Appendix 1.1, at the end of this chapter.

Schedule Mandatory Vacations and Rotate Employees

It is a good idea to establish mandatory vacations as part of the hotel's personnel policies. Aside from the human-resources issue, this policy has important internal control implications. Particularly for accounting, cash-handling, and other clerical employees, the idea that at some time in the year they must relinquish their work to someone else is a healthy one. It allows fresh perspectives to surface, and sometimes uncovers unhealthy or weak situations. In many cases of fraud and embezzlement, the discovery of the fraud took place when someone unexpectedly left his or her duties. Many of these cases of internal control failure appear throughout the book. That notion sounds detective rather than preventative, but if mandatory vacations are standard operating procedure, they will, indeed, be preventative.

A comparable procedure involves the rotation of employees where this is feasible. Cashier, clerk, and other clerical positions are generally good candidates for rotation. Some of the same benefits are obtained as those stemming from mandatory vacations. Additionally, the rotated employees have a chance to experience a wider sample of the hotel's operations. There are sometimes difficulties with rotation, since skill requirements are not necessarily interchangeable. Where practical, though, rotation is a useful part of an overall internal control program.

Conduct Frequent External Audits

It is essential to have frequent, independent audits performed by an external audit firm. The independence and objectivity brought to the audit process by an outside auditor are extremely valuable. It is also important for the top management of the hotel—the general manager and the controller, for example—to discuss the state of the hotel's internal controls with the outside auditors. As part of their audit process, outside auditors assess the general strength or weakness of the operation's internal controls. This assessment is one of the ways in which auditors determine the scope of their audit. It is a good idea for management to ask for feedback on that process, and to use that information to improve apparent weaknesses.

It is also important to recognize that having external audits means neither that the hotel is fraud-proof nor that all frauds and embezzlements will be discovered. The objectives of the outside auditor are much broader than fraud detection alone. Those objectives, the procedures, and the implications of audits—both external and internal—are discussed in greater detail later. Although outside audits do not guarantee that a hotel is fraud-proof, they are a strongly recommended part of the overall internal control program.

Use Cost-Benefit Analysis

This final principle is an important one: internal control programs must be subject to the same cost-benefit analysis as any other investment or part of the hotel operation. To be feasible, the cost of internal control procedures should be lower than their benefits. The problem with this type of analysis for internal control is that the benefits are hard to measure. The costs are usually fairly cut-and-dried, but the benefits are stated in terms of possible or anticipated losses prevented. If all works well, a hotel will experience no losses, yet it must estimate what fraud or embezzlement exposure it will face so as to project anticipated benefits of internal control. Cost-benefit analysis is essential because it is easy for internal control programs to run up high costs—particularly for the labor required to obtain proper division of duties and to maintain checks and balances. Management, therefore, must do its best to cost-justify all control programs.

The Scope of Internal Auditing

The term "internal auditing" is difficult to define, given the dramatic changes in this internal control function over the last two decades and differing corporate approaches toward it. This study has found that internal auditing has evolved into a broad field, involving many activities and responsibilities. Added to the more traditional roles of internal auditors—financial, operational, and compliance auditing, for example—internal auditors are taking on new responsibilities resulting from changes both inside and outside the corporation.

Among the most significant of these changes is the growing importance of the computer, which has provided internal auditors with both more areas to be audited (EDP auditing) and new tools to help them perform their jobs, such as computer-assisted auditing techniques (CAATS). Another significant change is the regulatory environment. New responsibilities for the internal auditor have resulted from changing Financial Accounting Standards Board (FASB) requirements, Securities and Exchange Commission (SEC) regulations, and auditing standards. Within the corporation, the growing respect for internal auditors has led many firms to rely heavily on the auditors' expertise. Internal consulting has become, for many internal auditors, another major area of responsibility.

Furthermore, the function of internal auditing varies considerably among corporations according to both company size and industry as well as specific corporate cultures. Nevertheless, to provide a framework for this report, the following definition of internal auditing as defined by the Institute of Internal Auditors in the Standards for the Professional Practice of Internal Auditing is offered: Internal auditing is an independent appraisal function established within an organization to examine and evaluate its activities as a service to the organization. The objective of internal auditing is to assist members of the organization in the effective discharge of their responsibilities. To this end, internal auditing furnishes them with analysis, appraisals, recommendations, counsel, and information concerning the activities reviewed.

Independence

Internal auditors must be independent of the activities they audit, and are so when they can carry out their work freely and objectively. Independence permits internal auditors to render the impartial and unbiased judgment essential to the proper conduct of the audit, and is achieved through organizational status and objectivity. Typically, the internal audit department will organizationally report to an individual outside of the daily operations.

Internal Audit Activities

Auditors and non-auditors often speak in terms of financial, operational, compliance, systems, and management auditing, but these terms have not been well defined. As one audit director sagely stated, "My recent experience with interviewing prospective candidates for audit manager and audit senior makes me skeptical that there is a clear understanding of what constitutes financial auditing and what is understood by operational auditing."

The box below classifies auditing activities and provides descriptions of them. Of course, the activities involved in a given audit objective or project will most often straddle more than one type of audit.

Classification of Internal Audit Activities

Auditing Activities	Descriptions
Financial Auditing	The review and testing of the reliability and integrity of financial information and the systems that deliver this information. It includes work done in support of the independent, external auditors.
Operational Auditing	A review of the economy, efficiency, and effectiveness of operations. It sometimes includes a broad review and evaluation of management performance with respect to the achievement of corporate goals.
Fraud Auditing	An audit specifically targeting irregularities, their magnitude, and the rate of their occurrence.
Compliance Auditing	The review and testing of the organization's compliance with statutory, regulatory, and internal policy requirements.
Computer Auditing	The review and testing of the computer systems that process financial and nonfinancial information to assure the integrity of this information.
Internal Consulting	This category includes non-audit activities. These are often one-time assignments and have been traditionally referred to as "special projects."

NOTE: This and portions of the preceding two pages were taken from the KPMG Peat Marwick publication *New Directions in Internal Auditing*.

The Smaller Company

In larger companies, the independence of the internal auditor or department is reinforced by reporting directly to the Audit Committee of the Board of Directors. With this reporting relationship, the auditor avoids the appearance of a lack of independence, since he or she is not responsible to operational management. In smaller companies, the auditor may report to a department manager, such as the chief financial officer. However, it is critical that the auditor have authority and the blessing of upper management to circumvent this reporting line if professionally necessary.

For smaller companies the cost of an internal auditor or audit department may not be justifiable. External auditors (CPA firms) will agree to perform the audit function. Additionally, selecting an appropriate person in the company to function as a part-time auditor may provide an acceptable level of oversight.

Endnotes

1. American Institute of Certified Public Accountants (AICPA), Committee on Auditing Procedure, Special Report, 1949.
2. See: Norman Jaspan, *The Thief in White Collar* (Philadelphia: J.B. Lippinocott, 1960).
3. See, for example: Raymond S. Schmidgall, *Hospitality Industry Managerial Accounting*, Third Edition (East Lansing, Mich.: Educational Institute of the American Hotel & Motel Association, 1995).

Front of House

Room Revenue

Room revenue represents the most significant revenue source in a hotel operation; in many hotels, it is the only source. Food and beverage operations and ancillary services are included in a hotel's operations to enhance the property's ability to maximize room revenue by attracting, retaining, and satisfying its guests.

Regardless of the size of the hotel, controls must be in place to ensure that 1) rooms are properly rented, 2) correct rates are charged for the rooms, 3) room-related charges are properly accumulated (including charges for ancillary services), and 4) ultimate payment for the rooms is secured.

Regardless of the size of the hotel, the objective is to maximize room revenue. This is generally accomplished through adopting a yield management strategy. In simple terms, this is the process of setting rates at the maximum level that can be attained during periods of heavy demand, and modifying rates or providing attractive ancillary benefits to attract incremental business when demand is low. Once these rates are determined, either through setting seasonal rack rates or through setting contract-term guidelines for convention or tour and travel group business, controls need to be set in place to ensure that the rates established by management are the rates that employees offer to the guests. This is a communication process that should provide documentation of acceptable rates and should also include a control to identify deviations from the designed rate structure. This is particularly significant if employees are empowered to offer alternative rates to entice a guest to stay with the hotel.

Once a guest is committed to stay with a hotel, a complex process is set in motion to ensure that the guest's stay is properly accounted for. Perhaps one of the most significant controls available is properly trained front desk personnel. If the front desk personnel do not obtain the proper information related to the guest, the ability to subsequently collect the charges related to the stay may be jeopardized. Controls should be established to ensure that the method of payment is identified upon registration so that the payment to the hotel is reasonably assured. This includes establishing criteria for advance deposits, preapproval of credit card charges, and, where appropriate, approval for direct billing through the city ledger.

The accumulation of charges can present problems if there are many sources of charges for services to the guests. Controls must be set in place to ensure that all rents from all occupied rooms are billed. This requires controls to monitor room status. Also, controls must be in place to facilitate the timely and accurate posting of charges to each room from the food and beverage outlets and other ancillary services utilized by the guest. Of particular concern is proper control over the authorization process related to rebates and allowances posted to guest accounts.

The ultimate goal is to provide the guest a room in an atmosphere that will make that stay an enjoyable experience and encourage the guest to return, while at the same time ensuring the hotel's ability to collect its fees without complications that would destroy guest relations. An effective set of internal controls is the key to success in meeting that goal.

The following outline of "Proposed Internal Controls for Room Revenue" and the related risk matrices are organized in their presentation to follow the flow of the revenue generation cycle, beginning with the establishment of appropriate pricing, and then addressing the occupancy process from acceptance of the guest reservation through check-out of the guest upon the conclusion of his or her stay.

Proposed Internal Controls for Room Revenue

Establishing Prices

Authorize room rates to be charged.
Communicate approved room rates to appropriate parties.
Authorize deviations from approved rates.

Accepting Reservations

Obtain complete and accurate reservation information.
Accept reservations in accordance with established policies.

Checking In the Guest

Receive reservation information in a timely manner.
Establish approved methods of payment.
Obtain necessary guest information.
Train front desk personnel.
Obtain evidence of guest check-in.
Maintain current room status information.

Recording Room Revenue

Bill all occupied rooms.
Post charges in a timely and accurate manner.
Provide a statement of charges to the guest.
Authorize rebates and allowances.

Checking Out the Guest

Close out guest records in the guest ledger.
Update the current room status.

Proposed Internal Controls for Room Revenue

Establishing Prices

Control	Risk If Control Is Not in Place	Example of Method to Achieve Control Objective
Authorize room rates to be charged.	• Room rates may not provide a sufficient profit margin, lowering the property's profits.	• Senior management should review and formally approve the rates to be charged.
Communicate approved room rates to appropriate parties.	• Incorrect rates may be quoted and charged to guests.	• Room rates should be communicated to employees and guests via published rate schedules and updates of rate information in reservation office and front desk systems.
Authorize deviations from approved rates.	• Rooms may be sold for rates below the rates authorized by management.	• Deviations from authorized rates should be approved by management or its designee.

Proposed Internal Controls for Room Revenue

Accepting Reservations

Control	Risk If Control Is Not in Place	Example of Method to Achieve Control Objective
Obtain complete and accurate reservation information.	• Duplicate reservations could be accepted.	• Use standard forms and procedures to record reservation information.
Accept reservations in accordance with established policies.	• The hotel may overbook reservations.	• Document policies and procedures for accepting reservations, requiring advance deposits, etc.

Proposed Internal Controls for Room Revenue

Checking In the Guest

Control	Risk If Control Is Not in Place	Example of Method to Achieve Control Objective
Receive reservation information in a timely manner.	• The guest may be inconvenienced by long check-in lines.	• Document the backup procedures to be used if automated systems are not functional.
Establish approved methods of payment.	• An excessive number of accounts may be uncollectible.	• Prepare written policies that clearly state approved methods of payment.
Obtain necessary guest information.	• Billing discrepancies may occur or guest accounts may be uncollectible.	• Establish standard guest registration procedures that specify the information to be obtained from each guest.
Train front desk personnel.	• The guest may be inconvenienced and billing errors may occur.	• Establish well-documented policies and procedures and adequate supervision.
Obtain evidence of guest check-in.	• Room charges may be disputed.	• Establish procedures requiring that all guests sign a standard registration form.
Maintain current room status information.	• The guest may be incorrectly advised that no room is available.	• Establish an automated front desk system that updates room status when a guest checks out and when housekeeping indicates a room is available for occupancy.

Proposed Internal Controls for Room Revenue

Recording Room Revenue

Control	Risk If Control Is Not in Place	Example of Method to Achieve Control Objective
Bill all occupied rooms.	• Revenue will be lost.	• Reconcile housekeeping's report of occupied rooms to guest registration records on a daily basis.
Post charges in a timely and accurate manner.	• The number of uncollectible charges will increase.	• Establish an automated system for posting room and outlet charges.
Provide a statement of charges to the guest.	• Billings will be disputed.	• Establish an automated front desk system that prints guest folios at checkout.
Authorize rebates and allowances.	• Incorrect revenue adjustments may be processed.	• Require management or its designee to approve adjustments.

Proposed Internal Controls for Room Revenue

Checking Out the Guest

Control	Risk If Control Is Not in Place	Example of Method to Achieve Control Objective
Close out guest records in the guest ledger.	• The guest may be billed for a vacant room.	• Promptly investigate any discrepancies between housekeeping occupancy records and front desk records.
Update the current room status.	• The check-in of arriving guests may be delayed.	• Establish an automated front desk system that updates room status when a previous guest checks out and when housekeeping indicates a room is available for occupancy.

Food and Beverage Revenue

Regardless of the size and number of food establishments a lodging property contains, certain basic control elements must exist in order to ensure that revenue is collected for all food and beverage sales. First, procedures must be established to ensure that sales are recorded for all food and beverages served to customers. Second, procedures must be established to ensure that food and beverages are sold at the correct prices. And finally, procedures must be established to ensure that all sales receipts are collected and recorded at the point of sale.

These three basic control processes are essential to any food and beverage service operation, from the smallest snack bar to the most sophisticated fine-dining restaurant, and they are encompassed in the control objectives and procedures outlined on the following pages.

In addition to basic accounting controls, the following pages include other control objectives that should be an integral part of any successful food or beverage operation. Of paramount importance is the establishment of guidelines regarding food and beverage quality and physical safety. Food-safety and alcohol-awareness training are critical elements of a properly designed control system. Other control elements necessary to the successful food and beverage operation include periodic checks and reviews of menu pricing and content; staff training programs; staffing guidelines; seating rotation procedures; inventory controls; and suggestive-selling processes and techniques.

Proposed Internal Controls for Food and Beverage Revenue

Planning and Pricing the Menu

Plan, price, and periodically update menu items and product lists.
Authorize prices to be charged.
Authorize officers' checks, complimentary meals, and discounts.
Document guest reservation procedures.
Establish staffing guidelines based on forecasted business.
Establish seating rotation procedures.
Establish and maintain adequate par stocks.
Establish and implement suggestive-selling techniques.
Establish and implement hospitality training programs.
Set up a shopping service—establish an independent review of guest service and control procedures.

Recording Revenue

Establish order/entry procedures, and train staff in the proper use of the POS system.
Authorize and account for void checks and transactions/adjustments.
Verify cash transactions and settlements.
Establish and maintain proper food and beverage check controls.
Prove the mathematical accuracy of F&B checks and verify the posting of revenues and settlements.
Calculate beverage sales potentials.
Independently control guest/cover counts.
Establish additional check controls for the restaurant buffet.
Audit banquet checks.
Establish procedures for banquet cash bars.
Balance, post, and verify all F&B transactions by Night and Income Audit.
Record minibar consumption daily.
Authorize steward sales.

Minimizing General Risks

Establish a food safety program.
Establish an alcohol awareness program.

Prepared/Submitted by: Susan J. Claremont, TCC
Mark Parr, Marriott

Proposed Internal Controls for Food and Beverage Revenue

Planning and Pricing the Menu

Control	Risk If Control Is Not in Place	Example of Method to Achieve Control Objective
Plan, price, and periodically update menu items and product lists.	• Revenue potential will not be maximized. • The market share and customer base will decrease.	• Initially cost and price all menu and product items to maximize revenue potential and obtain the desired cost percentage and product mix. • Periodically review each menu item to determine if the retail price based on food costs is marketable, and adjust prices accordingly. Based on forecasted market share and business volume, cost the entire menu to determine the overall potential food cost. • Perform the above steps for beverage costs compared to calculated potentials and forecasted volume.

Proposed Internal Controls for Food and Beverage Revenue

Planning and Pricing the Menu

Control	Risk If Control Is Not in Place	Example of Method to Achieve Control Objective
Authorize prices to be charged.	• Revenue may be misstated or lost, or funds may be misappropriated.	• Perform a quarterly analysis of each outlet's menus and, when possible, eliminate items that do not achieve the desired profitability and mix. Revise menus to reflect demand. • Maintain authorized price lists for all F&B items offered for sale. Program POS systems in accordance with authorized price lists. • Limit access to the POS price change function to authorized personnel. Require periodic, independent checks of POS PLM's and prices per F&B checks against the menu and price lists. • Restrict the use of miscellaneous keys, and authorize special-request items that have not been programmed before.
Authorize officers' checks, complimentary meals, and discounts.	• Revenue may be misstated or lost; funds may be misappropriated; costs may be overstated due to improper accounting for complimentary meals.	• Communicate authorization and restrictions on officers' checks to all outlets. Require management to authorize and support all other complimentary and discounted meals. Require discount and complimentary coupons to be secured, accounted for, and canceled upon redemption to prevent reuse.

Proposed Internal Controls for Food and Beverage Revenue

Planning and Pricing the Menu

Control	Risk If Control Is Not in Place	Example of Method to Achieve Control Objective
Document guest reservation procedures.	• Revenue may decrease and the guest may be dissatisfied.	• Put documented reservation procedures in effect and properly train all associates responsible for accepting reservations to perform procedures.
Establish staffing guidelines based on forecasted business.	• Revenue may decrease; the guest may be dissatisfied due to poor service; income may be lost due to overstaffing; costs may increase due to anticipated overtime.	• Document forecasted business and staff according to anticipated business demand.
Establish seating rotation procedures.	• Revenue may decrease; the guest may be dissatisfied.	• Implement a seating rotation policy to ensure that guest volume is adequately distributed and quality service is extended to all guests.
Establish and maintain adequate par stocks.	• Revenue may decrease because the desired product is unavailable.	• Establish and maintain pars for all required food and beverage ingredients. Adjust pars as business demands change.
Establish and implement suggestive-selling techniques.	• Revenue may decrease.	• Develop and implement training programs. Encourage servers to upsell.

Proposed Internal Controls for Food and Beverage Revenue

Planning and Pricing the Menu

Control	Risk If Control Is Not in Place	Example of Method to Achieve Control Objective
Establish and implement hospitality training programs.	• Revenue may decrease and the guest may be dissatisfied.	• Develop and maintain an ongoing hospitality/guest service training program.
Set up a shopping service—establish an independent review of guest service and control procedures.	• Revenue may decrease; funds may be pilfered and misappropriated; management may be unaware of the associates' conduct when not present.	• Utilize a shopping service to periodically spot-check F&B outlets and inform management of the staff's degree of adherence to company policies and procedures.

Proposed Internal Controls for Food and Beverage Revenue

Recording Revenue

Control	Risk If Control Is Not in Place	Example of Method to Achieve Control Objective
Establish order/entry procedures, and train staff in the proper use of the POS system.	• Revenue may be misstated or lost. • F&B costs may increase due to waste incurred by incorrect orders. • Cover counts or statistics and cost percentages may be incorrect due to misallocation or misclassification. • The guest may be dissatisfied; guest checks may be incorrect; the guest may receive the wrong check; the guest may be served something different from what is ordered.	• Enter orders as they are taken and communicated to the kitchen or bar. • Use pre-checks, the dupe/chit system, on-line kitchens, and service bar printers. • Use red-lining or bar checks for lounge sales. • Open beverage checks for each sale; ring them up as served; place them in front of customers seated at bars. • Use a unique coding of checks and server IDs. • Separate server and cashiering functions. • Require floor walkers and the bar manager to make the sure the check procedures of bar sales are followed. • Document policies and procedures; provide ongoing hands-on training and adequate supervision. • Establish and maintain appropriate system and function access levels, and properly control access keys.

Proposed Internal Controls for Food and Beverage Revenue

Recording Revenue

Control	Risk If Control Is Not in Place	Example of Method to Achieve Control Objective
Authorize and account for void checks and transactions/adjustments.	• Revenue may be misstated or lost; funds may be misappropriated; costs may be undetected; errors and irregularities may not be detected; adjustment transactions may not be authorized or accounted for.	• Require all voided items and checks to be authorized by management. • Restrict access to void/adjustment keys to management personnel. • Require cashiers and Income Audit to physically retain and account for void checks. • Require Income Audit to review void/adjustment logs and POS reports daily.
Verify cash transactions and settlements.	• Revenue may decrease; funds may be pilfered; errors and irregularities may be undetected.	• Perform periodic surprise counts of F&B cashier drawers. Reconcile cash settlements to recorded amounts per POS system.
Establish and maintain proper food and beverage check controls.	• Funds may be misappropriated due to reuse of guest checks; revenue may decrease or be lost due to orders not being recorded. • Open checks may be left in the system; settlements may not be collected or recorded.	• Secure and independently issue blank guest checks; require Income Audit to numerically control, account for, and verify checks issued and used. • Hold servers and cashiers accountable for checks issued, used, returned, and voided. • Lock boxes maintained at bars for control of cash checks immediately upon settlement. • Account for and settle open checks prior to the end of the shift.

Proposed Internal Controls for Food and Beverage Revenue

Recording Revenue

Control	Risk If Control Is Not in Place	Example of Method to Achieve Control Objective
Prove the mathematical accuracy of F&B checks and verify the posting of revenues and settlements.	• Revenue, sales tax, and gratuities may be misstated; revenue and settlements may not be captured; revenue may not be recorded in the correct period; orders taken and served may not be rung up and entered after the settlement is collected.	• Daily post F&B checks to guest accounts and ledger control accounts and ledger control (manual systems non-interfaced). • Verify that taxes and gratuities are properly entered into the POS system. • Verify that all checks are settled to a zero balance. • Re-add individual checks on a test basis (manual system only); prove tax/gratuity calculation; ensure that totals are allocated to the correct accounts (for example, food, beverage, miscellaneous revenue, tax, gratuity, etc.). • Prove or verify cumulative check revenue totals or settlement types against recorded amounts per system, the F&B recap, and the daily report. Verify settlements against checks or the PMS system. • Verify that checks have been closed to the correct settlement type and room charge checks have been closed to the correct rooms. • Verify dupes/chits; precheck, etc., to checks on test basis. • Require Night Audit to take "Z" readings and to verify them against recorded amounts and checks.

Proposed Internal Controls for Food and Beverage Revenue

Recording Revenue

Control	*Risk If Control Is Not in Place*	*Example of Method to Achieve Control Objective*
Calculate beverage sales potentials.	• Revenue may decrease or be pilfered.	• Based on actual consumption, calculate the outlet's potential sales compared with the actual sales recorded. Investigate material variances.
Independently control guest/cover counts.	• Revenue may decrease; the inability to detect the decline in average sales per cover may occur; statistics will be incorrect.	• Ensure that the host maintains a guest count based on the number of guests seated. Compare the host count to the number of guests served or rung up on the POS. Investigate any variances per check/guest meal counts (manual systems) or recorded amounts.
Establish additional check controls for the restaurant buffet.	• Revenue may decrease; revenue may be pilfered; funds may be misappropriated.	• Make sure the host controls and issues checks to the server as guests are seated. Perform a comparison between the number of guests seated times the buffet price and the amount of revenue recorded for the meal period.

Proposed Internal Controls for Food and Beverage Revenue

Recording Revenue

Control	Risk If Control Is Not in Place	Example of Method to Achieve Control Objective
Audit banquet checks.	• Revenue may be misstated or lost; charges may be inaccurate.	• Compare recorded amounts per sales check to contracted amounts per BEO/contract. • Verify the existence of authorization for price deviations. • Compare covers charged to guarantees and actual covers prepared and served. • Prove the mathematical accuracy of banquet checks including sales taxes and gratuities and the allocation of charges (for example, food, beverage, miscellaneous, etc.). • Review banquet checks for completeness and collection settlements in accordance with contracts. • Review and compare beverage charges to the banquet beverage requisition and consumption reports.
Establish procedures for banquet cash bars.	• Revenue may be misstated, lost, or pilfered; costs may be overstated; funds may be misappropriated.	• Calculate potential sales and compare them to recorded sales. • Separate bartending and cashiering functions. • Utilize tickets for the redemption of beverages purchased. • Maintain ticket control. • Calculate tickets used and verify them against tickets redeemed and revenue and cash collected.

Proposed Internal Controls for Food and Beverage Revenue

Recording Revenue

Control	Risk If Control Is Not in Place	Example of Method to Achieve Control Objective
Balance, post, and verify all F&B transactions by Night and Income Audit.	• Revenue or settlement may not be recorded or captured; the system may not be balanced; errors and irregularities may go undetected.	• Prepare daily F&B report and balancing to "Z" readings, F&B checks, hotel daily report, and settlement report. • Independently verify by an Income Audit and verification and the preparation of the daily hotel revenue journal.
Record minibar consumption daily.	• Revenue may be overstated by double posting of items consumed; revenue may be pilfered; revenue may be lost.	• Use preprinted checks to compare consumption and issues to recorded revenue. • Use automated minibar systems. • Forward charges to the front desk, posted timely. • Replenish and examine daily. • Maintain locks and seals on cabinets to control access. • Control keys.
Authorize steward sales.	• Revenue may be pilfered or unrecorded; costs may increase.	• Prepare authorized steward sales slips to support all transactions. Verify them by an Income Audit.

Proposed Internal Controls for Food and Beverage Revenue

Minimizing General Risks

Control	Risk If Control Is Not in Place	Example of Method to Achieve Control Objective
Establish a food safety program.	• Revenue may decrease as a result of negative publicity from a foodborne illness outbreak; a lawsuit may occur.	• Perform periodic inspections of the operation to ensure adherence to all Health Code Standards.
Establish an alcohol awareness program.	• Revenue may decrease as a result of the loss of the Liquor License; a lawsuit may occur.	• Perform periodic inspections to ensure that the operation adheres to state and local liquor laws.

Telephone Revenue

Internal control of the telephone system begins in the initial planning stages. It is important to select the telephone switch and the call-accounting vendor that are best suited to the operation. In most cases, it is not cost effective to change either the telephone switch or the call-accounting system after installation.

Control over the long-distance carrier needs to be reviewed regularly for cost and guest satisfaction. Along with this review, there should be a review of the markup margin to ensure that profit is maximized.

The long-distance invoice should be compared to revenue monthly in order to discover any problems, such as recording insufficient revenue or incurring unneeded expense.

Proposed Internal Controls for Telephone Revenue

Establishing Prices

Select a telephone switch.
Select a long-distance carrier and rate structure.
Select a call-accounting vendor.
Establish a markup margin.

Recording Revenue

Post charges in a timely and accurate manner.
Reconcile total charges daily from the call-accounting vendor report to the total posted telephone charges.
Establish procedures for operator-assisted calls.
Provide a statement of charges to the guest.
Authorize rebates and allowances.
Establish procedures for manual systems.
Restrict the outside operator without restricting 911 calls.

Reviewing the Long-Distance Invoice to Guest Charges

Review the markup margin.
Review potential operator-assisted calls (e.g., overseas, third-party charges) to guest postings.
Review for unusual charges (e.g., 900 numbers).
Review the Call-Accounting Configuration.
Review the Call-Accounting Database.

Proposed Internal Controls for Telephone Revenue

Establishing Prices

Control	Risk If Control Is Not in Place	Example of Method to Achieve Control Objective
Select a telephone switch.	• The system may be too large and not cost effective. The system may be too small and inefficient and unable to be expanded.	• Hire consultants to determine a system that meets the needs of the hotel.
Select a long-distance carrier and rate structure.	• Customer service may suffer due to poor connections. Rates paid to the carrier may not be the most cost-beneficial.	• Hire consultants to determine a system that meets the needs of the hotel.
Select a call-accounting vendor.	• The markup margin may not be correct due to poor customer service. Outgoing calls may not be routed in the most cost-efficient manner.	• Hire consultants to determine a system that meets the needs of the hotel.
Establish a markup margin.	• The markup margin may be too high, reducing outgoing volume. The margin may be too low, generating insufficient revenue.	• Approve the markup margin, and review the margin on a regular basis.

Proposed Internal Controls for Telephone Revenue

Recording Revenue

Control	Risk If Control Is Not in Place	Example of Method to Achieve Control Objective
Post charges in a timely and accurate manner.	Revenue may be lost.	Establish an automated system for posting charges. Activate and deactivate room phones from PBX.
Reconcile total charges daily from the call-accounting vendor report to the total posted charges.	Revenue may be lost.	Have the front desk shift its balancing procedures to include reconciling the call-accounting report to shift postings.
Establish procedures for operator-assisted calls.	Revenue may be lost.	Include procedures in the training of front desk clerks and PBX operators.
Provide a statement of charges to the guest.	Billings may be disputed.	Indicate the date, time, and phone number called on the guest folio.
Authorize rebates and allowances.	Incorrect revenue adjustments may be processed.	Require adjustments to be approved by management or its designees.
Establish procedures for manual systems.	Revenue may be lost.	Require the long-distance log or daily tally sheet to be compared to daily folio postings.
Restrict the outside operator without restricting 911 calls.	Revenue may be lost. Expenses may be excessive.	Restrict the outside operator through Call-Accounting Configuration.

Proposed Internal Controls for Telephone Revenue

Reviewing the Long-Distance Invoice to Guest Charges

Control	Risk If Control Is Not in Place	Example of Method to Achieve Control Objective
Review the markup margin.	• Revenue may be lost. Customers may complain of excessive rates.	• Compare overall revenue with long-distance expenses for reasonableness. Compare sample rates from the long-distance invoice with specific guest charges.
Review potential operator-assisted calls (e.g., overseas, third-party charges) to guest postings.	• Revenue may be lost. Expenses may increase.	• Reconcile to call-accounting either the entire long-distance invoice or a sample of overseas and third-party calls.
Review for unusual charges (e.g., 900 numbers).	• Revenue may be lost. Expenses may increase.	• Review the telephone invoice for charges not associated with guest or administrative charges.
Review the Call-Accounting Configuration.	• Revenue may be lost.	• Compare the vendor invoice to guest postings.
Review the Call-Accounting Database.	• Revenue may be lost.	• Compare the vendor invoice to guest postings.

Other Revenue

Controls for other revenue are divided into two types—those provided internally (in-house) and those provided by outside vendors.

The decision to provide a service in-house or to go outside is an important one. It needs to be reevaluated on a regular basis to determine if conditions have altered significantly enough to warrant changing the original decision.

For either case, it is important to associate the appropriate expense with the corresponding revenue. This gives the proprietor the necessary tools to review markup rates on a regular basis.

For services provided internally, it is important that personnel are properly trained. For services provided by external vendors, a signed contract that details the commission rate and the method for recording charges and settling guest disputes is important.

Proposed Internal Controls for Other Revenue

Services Provided by an External Vendor

Selecting Services and Vendors

Determine whether to provide service internally or contract outside the hotel.
Authorize a vendor.
Obtain a written contract with the vendor.
Establish a commission rate.
Review the vendor's insurance limits.

Recording Revenue

Establish procedures for how charges will be accepted from the vendor.
Post charges in a timely and accurate manner.
Provide a statement of charges to the guest.
Authorize rebates and allowances.

Reviewing the Vendor Invoice to Guest Charges

Reconcile the vendor invoice to guest postings and allowances.
Review the commission rate for accuracy.
Audit concessionaires and outside vendors.
Ensure that the vendor has the necessary licenses and permits.

Services Provided Internally

Establishing Prices

Select a recording method for sales and receipts (e.g., separate outlet or all through the front desk).
Develop a system to accumulate applicable expenses.
Authorize rates to be charged for services.

Recording Revenue

Bill all applicable services.
Post charges in a timely and accurate manner.
Provide a statement of charges to the guest.
Authorize rebates and allowances.

Controlling Expenses

Train appropriate personnel.
Compare revenue with related expenses.

Proposed Internal Controls for Other Revenue

Services Provided by an External Vendor

Selecting Services and Vendors

Control	Risk If Control Is Not in Place	Example of Method to Achieve Control Objective
Determine whether to provide service internally or contract outside the hotel.	Customer service may be poor. Expenses may increase.	Make sure management reviews the cost analysis.
Authorize a vendor.	The customer may be dissatisfied. Revenue may be lost from commission.	Approve a vendor list.
Obtain a written contract with the vendor.	Billing, commission, and liability problems could develop from oral agreements.	Require attorneys to approve all contracts.
Establish a commission rate.	Revenue may be lost.	Make sure management approves the commission rate.
Review the vendor's insurance limits.	Potential liability for vendor negligence could cause excessive expense.	Require vendors to provide proof of insurance to limits prescribed by hotel management.

Proposed Internal Controls for Other Revenue

Services Provided by an External Vendor

Recording Revenue

Control	Risk If Control Is Not in Place	Example of Method to Achieve Control Objective
Establish procedures for how charges will be accepted from the vendor.	• Revenue may be lost, and vendor invoicing problems may occur.	• Use standard forms; require a guest signature before recording revenue.
Post charges in a timely and accurate manner.	• Revenue may be lost, and vendor invoicing problems may occur.	• Prenumber standard forms. Daily reconcile the vendor invoice (if available) to the guest charges.
Provide a statement of charges to the guest.	• Billings may be disputed.	• Retain a copy of the charge at the Front Desk until the guest checks out.
Authorize rebates and allowances.	• Revenue may be lost, and vendor invoicing problems may occur.	• Require management or its designees to approve adjustments.

Proposed Internal Controls for Other Revenue

Services Provided by an External Vendor

Reviewing the Vendor Invoice to Guest Charges

Control	Risk If Control Is Not in Place	Example of Method to Achieve Control Objective
Reconcile the vendor invoice to guest postings and allowances.	Expenses may be excessive.	Review the reconciliation of the vendor invoice to guest postings.
Review the commission rate for accuracy.	Revenue may be lost.	Approve the vendor invoice prior to payment.
Audit concessionaires and outside vendors.	Revenue may be lost.	Require the right to audit to be included in the contract.
Ensure that the vendor has the necessary licenses and permits.	Legal problems may occur.	Require the vendor to prove that the proper licenses and permits have been properly obtained and renewed.

Proposed Internal Controls for Other Revenue

Services Provided Internally

Establishing Prices

Control	Risk If Control Is Not in Place	Example of Method to Achieve Control Objective
Select a recording method for sales and receipts (e.g., separate outlet or all through the front desk).	Expenses may be excessive due to cost inefficiencies.	• Document policies and procedures for recording revenue and collecting receipts.
Develop a system to accumulate applicable expenses.	The price and markup margins may be incorrectly set; incorrect costs may be used for periodic evaluation.	• Document policies and procedures for recording expenses.
Authorize rates to be charged for services.	Rates may not provide a sufficient profit margin to justify providing services internally.	• Management must review and approve the rates to be charged.

Proposed Internal Controls for Other Revenue

Services Provided Internally

Recording Revenue

Control	Risk If Control Is Not in Place	Example of Method to Achieve Control Objective
Bill all applicable services.	• Revenue may be lost.	• Establish a policy of using prenumbered forms.
Post charges in a timely and accurate manner.	• Revenue may be lost.	• Post charges directly to the guest folio at the time of the charge, by phone or through a computer interface.
Provide a statement of charges to the guest.	• Billings may be disputed.	• Retain a copy of the charge at the front desk until the guest checks out.
Authorize rebates and allowances.	• Revenue may be lost and vendor invoicing problems may occur.	• Require management or its designees to approve adjustments.

Proposed Internal Controls for Other Revenue

Services Provided Internally

Controlling Expenses

Control	Risk If Control Is Not in Place	Example of Method to Achieve Control Objective
Train appropriate personnel.	• The guest may be inconvenienced by excessive expenses.	• Establish comprehensive job descriptions and documented training procedures.
Compare revenue with related expenses.	• Expenses may be excessive. Rates may be either excessive or insufficient to justify an internal decision.	• Complete a profit and loss report for each revenue center.

Cashiering
Proposed Internal Controls for Cashiering

Maintaining Cash Receipts—House Fund

Provide a secure storage area.
Limit access to cash monies.
Define the terms and conditions for maintenance of the house fund.
Establish accountability for the house fund.
Perform periodic, independent bank counts.

Maintaining Cash Receipts—Cash Banks

Provide a secure storage area.
Limit access to cash monies.
Define the terms and conditions for maintenance of cash banks.
Establish accountability for operating banks.
Perform periodic, independent bank counts.

Maintaining Cash Receipts—Cash Transactions

Post all guest payments immediately upon receipt.
Establish a check log for checks received in the mail.
Establish accountability.
Provide receipts for payments on accounts to guests.

Maintaining Cash Receipts—Check Cashing

Establish standards for check-cashing approval.
Establish check-cashing procedures.
Train cashiers to be alert to characteristics that may indicate a bad check.

Maintaining Cash Receipts—Petty Cash

Define criteria for the use of petty cash.
Establish standards for authorizing the use of petty cash.
Record the payment of petty cash.
Record expenses represented by petty cash payments on a timely basis.

Maintaining Cash Receipts—Paid Outs

Establish standards authorizing a paid out.
Establish accountability.
Post all paid outs in a timely and accurate manner.

Maintaining Cash Receipts—Deposits

Establish a system of deposits.
Establish accountability.
Ensure the accuracy and timeliness of cash deposits.
Account for and secure cash deposits.

Maintaining Cash Receipts—Check Payments

Accept checks for payment of accounts, advance deposits, and miscellaneous income in accordance with established policies.

Post check payments in a timely and accurate manner.

Provide a credited folio as a receipt of payment to the guest.

Maintaining Cash Receipts—Credit Card Transactions

Apply all credit card payments to guest accounts.

Approve credit cards.

Post payments in a timely and accurate manner.

Provide a credited folio as a receipt of payment to the guest.

Controlling Food and Beverage Revenue

Bill all food and beverage charges.

Post charges in a timely and accurate manner.

Provide a statement of charges to the guest.

Controlling Banquet and Meeting Room Revenue

Bill all banquet and meeting room charges.

Post charges in a timely and accurate manner.

Provide a statement of charges to the guest.

Controlling Miscellaneous Revenue

Bill all miscellaneous charges.

Post charges in a timely and accurate manner.

Provide a statement of charges to the guest.

Controlling Adjustments

Authorize all adjustments.

Post all adjustments in a timely and accurate manner.

Proposed Internal Controls for Cashiering

Maintaining Cash Receipts—House Fund

Control	Risk If Control Is Not in Place	Example of Method to Achieve Control Objective
Provide a secure storage area.	• Cash may be lost.	• Provide a safe for storage of cash monies.
Limit access to cash monies.	• Cash may be lost without recourse.	• Make sure the general manager or his or her designee knows the complete safe combination. • Change the safe combination periodically, and change it immediately if there have been personnel changes affecting staff members in possession of the safe combination or if there is reason to believe the safe combination has been compromised.
Define the terms and conditions for maintenance of the house fund.	• Cash monies may be used for purposes that do not meet management's criteria.	• Include all maintenance requirements in the contract bank form used to establish responsibility.
Establish accountability for the house fund.	• Cash may be lost without recourse.	• Make sure the general manager or his or her designee signs a contract establishing responsibility for the amount of the fund.
Perform periodic, independent bank counts.	• Unrecognized cash losses may occur.	• Require the bank to be counted by management staff on an unscheduled basis.

Proposed Internal Controls for Cashiering

Maintaining Cash Receipts—Cash Banks

Control	Risk If Control Is Not in Place	Example of Method to Achieve Control Objective
Provide a secure storage area.	• Cash may be lost.	• Provide a safety deposit box for the storage of monies.
Limit access to cash monies.	• Cash may be lost without recourse.	• Do not maintain duplicate safety deposit box keys. • Provide cash drawers that lock when they are not in use. • Do not allow multiple staff members to work out of the same cash drawer.
Define the terms and conditions for maintenance of cash banks.	• Cash monies may be used for purposes that do not meet management's criteria.	• Include all maintenance requirements in the contract bank form used to establish responsibility. • Do not allow cashiers to borrow funds from each other without management authorization and proper documentation.
Establish accountability for operating banks.	• Cash may be lost without recourse.	• Issue a contract bank to staff members handling cash transactions.
Perform periodic, independent bank counts.	• Unrecognized cash losses may occur.	• Require the bank to be counted by management staff on an unscheduled basis.

Proposed Internal Controls for Cashiering

Maintaining Cash Receipts—Cash Transactions

Control	Risk If Control Is Not in Place	Example of Method to Achieve Control Objective
Post all guest payments immediately upon receipt.	• Unrecognized cash losses and customer disputes may occur.	• Reconcile the cash drawer total to supporting documentation and the front office register reading at the end of each shift.
Establish a check log for checks received in the mail.	• Unrecognized cash losses and customer disputes may occur.	• Reconcile the check log to the posting and the certified deposit record.
Establish accountability.	• Cash may be lost without recourse.	• Install a front office register or computerized system that logs all cash transactions by the cashier.
Provide receipts for payments on accounts to guests.	• Cash may be misappropriated.	• Install an automated front office register system that logs all cash transactions and provides a receipt.

Proposed Internal Controls for Cashiering

Maintaining Cash Receipts—Check Cashing

Control	Risk If Control Is Not in Place	Example of Method to Achieve Control Objective
Establish standards for check-cashing approval.	• Bad check writeoffs may increase.	• Establish written policies that clearly state the criteria for check-cashing approval (must be a guest, etc.).
Establish check-cashing procedures.	• Bad check writeoffs may increase.	• Establish written policies that clearly state the information to be obtained and denoted on each check cashed.
Train cashiers to be alert to characteristics that may indicate a bad check.	• Bad check writeoffs may increase.	• Create a written summary of specific characteristics to look for when cashing checks.

Proposed Internal Controls for Cashiering

Maintaining Cash Receipts—Petty Cash

Control	Risk If Control Is Not in Place	Example of Method to Achieve Control Objective
Define criteria for the use of petty cash.	• Petty cash may be used for circumstances that do not meet management's criteria.	• Establish written requirements that clearly state the criteria for the use of petty cash.
Establish standards for authorizing the use of petty cash.	• Petty cash may be used for improper purposes.	• Require management approval of all petty-cash transactions.
Record the payment of petty cash.	• Unrecognized cash losses may occur.	• Require the completion of a petty-cash voucher. The voucher should contain all the information necessary to properly expense the payment: the cashier's name; management approval; and the signature of the staff member receiving payment.
Record expenses represented by petty-cash payments on a timely basis.	• Expenses may not be recorded in the proper accounting period.	• Require petty cash to be deposited with cash receipts on a daily basis.

Proposed Internal Controls for Cashiering

Maintaining Cash Receipts—Paid Outs

Control	Risk If Control Is Not in Place	Example of Method to Achieve Control Objective
Establish standards authorizing a paid out.	• Paid outs that do not meet management's criteria may be processed.	• Establish written policies that clearly state the criteria for paid outs.
Establish accountability.	• Paid outs may be processed without management's knowledge.	• Install a front office register or computerized system that logs all paid-out transactions by the cashier.
Post all paid outs in a timely and accurate manner.	• Unrecognized cash losses and customer disputes may occur.	• Require the use of a paid-out voucher as supporting documentation. The voucher should contain the guest's name, the guest's room number, an explanation, the cashier's name, and the guest's signature. • Attach all supporting documentation. • Reconcile cashier and night audit vouchers to register readings.

Proposed Internal Controls for Cashiering

Maintaining Cash Receipts—Deposits

Control	Risk If Control Is Not in Place	Example of Method to Achieve Control Objective
Establish a system of deposits.	• Unrecognized cash losses may occur.	• Establish written procedures that detail how a deposit is to be prepared.
Establish accountability.	• Cash losses may occur without recourse.	• Install a front office register or computerized system that logs all cash transactions by the cashier.
Ensure the accuracy and timeliness of cash deposits.	• Cash variances or losses may go unrecognized.	• Reconcile and deposit the cashier's cash receipts at the end of each shift. • Perform a cashiers' night audit reconciliation of the cash receipts and the total for each day.
Account for and secure cash deposits.	• Cash losses may occur.	• Require all deposits to be witnessed and listed on a deposit log before depositing them in a safe. • The general cashier or a designated employee must count and reconcile all deposits with the cash receipts journal on a daily basis.

Proposed Internal Controls for Cashiering

Maintaining Cash Receipts—Check Payments

Control	Risk If Control Is Not in Place	Example of Method to Achieve Control Objective
Accept checks for payment of accounts, advance deposits, and miscellaneous income in accordance with established policies.	• Bad debt expense or revenue loss may increase.	• Establish written policies that clearly state the criteria for accepting checks in payment of accounts and for recording advance deposits and miscellaneous revenue.
Post check payments in a timely and accurate manner.	• Billing may be disputed.	• Implement an automated system for posting payments to guest accounts.
Provide a credited folio as a receipt of payment to the guest.	• Payments may be improperly applied, resulting in guest disputes.	• Install a front office register or computerized system that logs all payments on guest accounts.

Proposed Internal Controls for Cashiering

Maintaining Cash Receipts— Credit Card Transactions

Control	Risk If Control Is Not in Place	Example of Method to Achieve Control Objective
Apply all credit card payments to guest accounts.	• Customer disputes and delayed payments may occur.	• Require guests to indicate the method of payment on their registration card. • Reconcile cashier and night audit checkout folios to credit card vouchers.
Approve credit cards.	• An increase in bad debt expense and delayed payments may occur.	• Establish the approval of credit cards through an online card approval service.
Post payments in a timely and accurate manner.	• Customer disputes and delayed payments may occur.	• Install an automated system for posting payments to guest accounts. • Reconcile cashier and night audit credit card payments to register readings.
Provide a credited folio as a receipt of payment to the guest.	• Payments may be improperly applied, resulting in guest disputes.	• Install a front office register or computerized system that logs all payments on guest accounts.

Proposed Internal Controls for Cashiering

Controlling Food and Beverage Revenue

Control	Risk If Control Is Not in Place	Example of Method to Achieve Control Objective
Bill all food and beverage charges.	• Revenue may be lost.	• Reconcile food and beverage check totals to front office register readings. • Reconcile food and beverage register readings to front office register readings.
Post charges in a timely and accurate manner.	• The guest may dispute charges, resulting in lost revenue or payment delays.	• Forward food and beverage checks to the front office for posting to guest accounts. • Reconcile food and beverage check totals to front office register totals.
Provide a statement of charges to the guest.	• Erroneous billings may go unnoticed.	• Maintain guest folios detailing charges.

Proposed Internal Controls for Cashiering

Controlling Banquet and Meeting Room Revenue

Control	Risk If Control Is Not in Place	Example of Method to Achieve Control Objective
Bill all banquet and meeting room charges.	• Revenue may be lost.	• Reconcile banquet check totals to front office register readings. • Reconcile the banquet summary to front office register readings.
Post charges in a timely and accurate manner.	• The guest may dispute charges, resulting in lost revenue or payment delays.	• Complete banquet checks for all charges. • Reconcile banquet check totals to front office register readings.
Provide a statement of charges to the guest.	• Erroneous billings may go unnoticed.	• Maintain guest folios detailing charges.

Proposed Internal Controls for Cashiering

Controlling Miscellaneous Revenue

Control	Risk If Control Is Not in Place	Example of Method to Achieve Control Objective
Bill all miscellaneous charges.	• Revenue may be lost.	• Reconcile an independently generated summary of charges to front desk postings. • Separate the posting function from the generation of charges.
Post charges in a timely and accurate manner.	• The guest may dispute charges, resulting in lost revenue or payment delays.	• Use charge slips for all miscellaneous guest charges. • Reconcile charge slips to front office desk postings.
Provide a statement of charges to the guest.	• Erroneous billings may go unnoticed.	• Maintain guest folios detailing charges.

Proposed Internal Controls for Cashiering

Controlling Adjustments

Control	Risk If Control Is Not in Place	Example of Method to Achieve Control Objective
Authorize all adjustments.	• Improper or incorrect adjustments may be processed.	• Require adjustments to be approved by management or its designee.
Post all adjustments in a timely and accurate manner.	• Under- or overstated revenues and guest disputes may occur.	• Use adjustment slips as supporting documentation. • Reconcile cashier and night audit adjustment slips to register readings.

Back of House

Purchasing

The size and complexity of a hotel's purchasing system varies directly with the size and complexity of the property. A large property with multiple food and beverage outlets and other ancillary services such as golf, tennis, or spa will require a more sophisticated purchasing system than will a 100-room motel serving the overnight business or pleasure traveler. However, the basic internal control objectives of the ordering, receiving, and payment functions remain the same for a large property or a small one.

A hotel's purchasing system should meet the following objectives:

- Authorize the specifications of goods and services required.
- Authorize the most appropriate vendor.
- Authorize and document the order to purchase.
- Verify that goods and services are received and/or provided as ordered.
- Authorize the payment for goods and services.
- Ensure that purchases are recorded in the appropriate accounting period and are appropriately classified in the financial statement.

The following examples of internal controls are designed to achieve these objectives, minimizing the risk of misappropriation of goods, services, and/or cash by unauthorized personnel.

Proposed Internal Controls for Purchasing

Ordering

Establish and authorize purchase specifications.
Communicate requirements to vendors.
Select the optimal vendor(s) and establish bid procedures.
Implement the use of authorized purchase orders or contracts, and requests.
Establish and maintain purchase procedures.

Receiving

Advise the receiver as to the goods expected.
Check the quality and quantity of goods or services received.
Record the receipt of goods or services and establish procedures for errors, returns, and goods received without invoice.
Communicate the receipt to stores and accounts payable.
Match the receiver's report and related purchase documentation.

Paying Vendors

Ensure that purchases are properly recorded, valued, classified, and accounted for.
Authorize the disbursement voucher.
Restrict access to critical forms, records, and processing areas.
Ensure that cash disbursements are valid, accounted for, properly recorded, in the correct amount, and classified.

Prepared/Submitted by: Susan J. Claremont, TCC
                         Peter Remek, Four Seasons

Proposed Internal Controls for Purchasing

Ordering

Control	Risk If Control Is Not in Place	Example of Method to Achieve Control Objective
Establish and authorize purchase specifications.	• The hotel may buy an inferior-quality product or the wrong product.	• Require senior management or the purchasing committee to review and approve all purchase and vendor specifications.
Communicate requirements to vendors.	• The hotel may receive goods that do not meet specifications.	• Communicate the hotel's written specifications to vendors.
Select the optimal vendor(s) and establish bid procedures.	• The hotel may not be getting the best possible quality or price.	• Require management to approve all new suppliers; obtain and document two to three bids; and perform market surveys.

Proposed Internal Controls for Purchasing

Ordering

Control	Risk If Control Is Not in Place	Example of Method to Achieve Control Objective
Implement the use of authorized purchase orders or contracts, and requests.	• Goods and services that are not needed may be ordered; this could result in write-downs of unusable or unsalable inventories. • Goods and services that do not meet authorized quality standards may be ordered. • Prices may be too high.	• Require all purchases to be approved in advance by management. • Establish the use of multipart, numerically controlled documents that are to be distributed to the vendor, the preparer, the department head, receiving, and accounting (accounts payable or cost control). • Establish the use of standard forms and formats.
Establish and maintain purchasing procedures.	• Transactions may be processed incorrectly.	• Create a policy-and-procedure manual and require adequate training and supervision.

Proposed Internal Controls for Purchasing

Receiving

Control	Risk If Control Is Not in Place	Example of Method to Achieve Control Objective
Advise the receiver as to the goods expected.	• Goods that were not ordered may be accepted; this could result in excessive inventory levels. • Goods may be invoiced or paid for without being received.	• Require order sheets and purchase orders to be made available to the receiver on a timely basis. • Require that procedures for rejecting goods that are not on the order sheet or purchase order be enforced.

Check the quality and quantity of goods or services received.	• Excessive quantities, incorrect items, or goods with unacceptable quality specifications may be received rather than refused or returned; this could result in excessive inventories.
	• The hotel may be paying for undetected shortages.
		• Give the receiver the following:
		  • A copy of standard specifications;
		  • Food and beverage order sheets and purchase orders; and
		  • An accurate scale.
		• Prior to accepting merchandise, carefully weigh or inspect it, and check it against the specifications of the approved purchase order and delivery note or invoice.

Proposed Internal Controls for Purchasing

Receiving

Control	Risk If Control Is Not in Place	Example of Method to Achieve Control Objective
Record the receipt of goods or services and establish procedures for errors, returns, and goods received without invoice.	• Goods may be received but not recorded and reported; this could result in a misstatement of inventory and cost sales and in unrecorded liabilities. • Returns may not be credited.	• Require the use of a receiving stamp and initialing and dating as evidence of receipt. • Require the use of prenumbered receiving documents. • Establish accounting procedures to ensure the correct sequence of receiving documents and an accurate follow-up of missing documents. • Require the follow-up of long-outstanding, unmatched orders. • Require the use of "Goods Received without Invoice," "Credit Memos," and "Notice of Error Correction" forms.
Communicate the receipt to stores and accounts payable.	• Goods may be lost or not forwarded to the storeroom on a timely basis.	• Require the storekeeper and cost control (or accounts payable) to receive a copy of the Daily Receiver's Report. • For food and beverage, require cost control to verify and cost items received; update inventory records, where applicable; and forward the receiving report, attached invoices, and other related documents to accounts payable for processing.

Proposed Internal Controls for Purchasing

Receiving

Control	Risk If Control Is Not in Place	Example of Method to Achieve Control Objective
Match the receiver's report and related purchase documentation.	• Unauthorized purchases may be processed for payment.	• Require the verification of quantities billed with receiving documents and purchase orders by persons other than those who prepare purchase orders or receiving records.

Proposed Internal Controls for Purchasing

Paying Vendors

Control

Ensure that purchases are properly recorded, valued, classified, and accounted for.

Risk If Control Is Not in Place

- Recorded purchases may be incorrectly valued.
- Recorded purchases may be improperly classified.
- Purchases may be recorded in the wrong period.
- Purchases may not be recorded.

Example of Method to Achieve Control Objective

- Require the internal verification of calculations and amounts.
- Investigate price variances between the purchase order and the invoice.
- Require an adequate chart of accounts and an internal review and verification of accounts distribution.
- Require the timely recording of transactions.
- Require the proper cutoff of goods and invoices received at month-end.
- Monthly reconcile vendor invoices to vendor statements; investigate outstanding items.
- Reconcile supporting journals and subsidiary ledgers to the general ledger control totals and account balances.
- Establish an accounts payable voucher system for the processing of all invoices through accounts payable.

Proposed Internal Controls for Purchasing

Paying Vendors

Control	Risk If Control Is Not in Place	Example of Method to Achieve Control Objective
Authorize the disbursement voucher.	• Payments may be made to nonexistent suppliers. • Incorrect or duplicate payments may be made.	• Require checks and check requisitions to be approved and signed by authorized personnel, and require specific and general authorizations for all payments. • Verify the accuracy of the vendor's invoices and supporting documents. • Require the verification of purchases and payment authorization prior to signing checks. • Require the authorization of check signers and the approval of payment when checks are signed.
Restrict access to critical forms, records, and processing areas.	• Records may be lost, destroyed, misused, or altered. • Unauthorized orders or payments may be made. • Payments for goods or services may not actually be received.	• Require the controlled custody of critical forms such as blank checks and purchase orders. • Separate the duties for accounts payable from the custody and mailing of signed checks.

Proposed Internal Controls for Purchasing

Paying Vendors

Control	Risk If Control Is Not in Place	Example of Method to Achieve Control Objective
Ensure that cash disbursements are valid, accounted for, properly recorded, in the correct amount, and classified.	• Cash disbursements may not be recorded. • Recorded cash disbursements may be improperly valued. • Recorded cash disbursements may be improperly classified. • Cash disbursements may be recorded in the wrong period. • Cash disbursement transactions may be improperly recorded or summarized and may not reconcile to items subsequently cleared by the bank.	• Make sure checks are prenumbered and accounted for. • Require the bank reconciliation to be performed monthly, independent of the recorded cash disbursements, accounts payable, or the custody of assets. • Require the internal verification of calculations and amounts. • Establish an adequate chart of accounts. • Ensure the timely recording of cash disbursements. • Establish the separation of the duties of purchasing, accounts payable, and the custody or mailing of signed checks. • Require the reconciliation of supporting journals and ledgers to the general ledger. • Establish the cancellation of the voucher package (invoice, receiving report, purchase order, etc.).

Inventories

The internal control of inventoried items should provide for the physical security (or safeguarding) and accountability of these items.

To achieve the goal of safeguarding, procedures should be designed to control the levels of inventory as well as their cost and the periodic physical counting.

Inventorial items should include operating supplies as well as perishable goods and other salable items. Management must receive accurate accounting, on a timely basis, of inventorial items to manage costs through budgets or pars and to match inventory levels to expected revenue and cash flow.

Proposed Internal Controls for Inventories

Controlling the Storeroom

Establish storeroom controls for inventory items (based on the size of the hotel and the availability of sufficient storage space).

- Food and beverage
- General supplies
- Guest supplies
- Engineering supplies
- Operating equipment (noncirculating)
  - China
  - Glass
  - Silver
  - Linen

Use forms and procedures to record the receipt and issue of inventory stores.
Maintain physical protection; safeguard assets.

Controlling Inventory Count and Valuation

Perform an inventory count and adjust physical records accordingly; ascertain the reasons for the differences. Reconcile the perpetual record to the general ledger control account monthly, where applicable.

Controlling Operating Equipment

Establish a procedure for the control of and accounting for reserve and in-use operating equipment.

Prepared/Submitted by: Susan J. Claremont, TCC

Proposed Internal Controls for Inventories

Controlling the Storeroom

Control	Risk If Control Is Not in Place	Example of Method to Achieve Control Objective
Establish storeroom controls for inventory items (based on the size of the hotel and the availability of sufficient storage space).	• Costs may be excessive. • Spoilage may occur. • Supply may not equal demand. • Inventory levels may be excessive. • Pilferage or misappropriation may occur.	• Post all items to a daily receiving record upon receipt. • Weigh food items and mark their weight and receipt date, as applicable.
• Food and beverage		• Price items (food stores, etc.) to facilitate pricing of requisitions and inventory.
• General supplies		• Establish minimum and maximum inventory levels and reorder points.
• Guest supplies		• Organize storerooms neatly and label bins clearly.
• Engineering supplies		• Post storeroom hours; restrict access.

• Operating equipment (noncirculating)
  • China
  • Glass
  • Silver
  • Linen
		• Authorize requisitions; require the general manager to approve the name/signature list and post it in the storeroom.
		• Maintain proper storeroom key control.
		• Establish and maintain insurance requirements.

Proposed Internal Controls for Inventories

Controlling the Storeroom

Control	Risk If Control Is Not in Place	Example of Method to Achieve Control Objective
Use forms and procedures to record the receipt and issue of inventory stores.	• Unauthorized purchases or issues may occur. • Theft or misappropriation may occur. • Costs may be over- or understated. • Unexplained variances between the ledger and the actual inventory may occur.	• Post all items to the daily receiving record upon receipt. • Require the authorized requisition to support all issues (see food and beverage cost control). • Maintain and update perpetual inventory records upon receipt and issue (where applicable). • Separate receiving, storekeeping, and recordkeeping functions. • Perform physical inventories in a timely manner and reconcile them to perpetual records. • Properly allocate the cost of issues to the operating department.
Maintain physical protection; safeguard assets.	• Unauthorized purchase or issues may occur. • Theft or misappropriation may occur. • Costs may be over- or understated. • Unexplained variances between the ledger and the actual inventory may occur.	• Lock areas (surveillance; security) as appropriate. • Restrict access; use documents requiring specific approvals. • Separate storekeeping and recordkeeping functions.

Proposed Internal Controls for Inventories

Controlling Inventory Count and Valuation

Control	Risk If Control Is Not in Place	Example of Method to Achieve Control Objective
Perform an inventory count and adjust physical records accordingly; ascertain the reasons for the differences. Reconcile the perpetual record to the general ledger control account monthly, where applicable.	• Unexplained or undetected variances between the ledger and the actual inventory may occur. • Undetected pilferage or theft may occur. • Assets may be over- or understated. • Costs may be over- or understated. • Excessive purchases or overstocking may occur. • Supply may be insufficient to meet the demand or operating requirements. • An insufficient amount of inventory may lead to uneconomical purchasing practices and increased costs.	• Develop a schedule, written procedures, and instructions for a physical count. • Ensure a proper cutoff; all deliveries for the day should be received and stored and issues should be completed (or deliveries separated from the inventory until the count is completed). • Post receipts and issues soon after receiving them. • Neatly organize storerooms, and clearly label bins. • Clearly identify units, counts, and quantities (product type, code, unit of measure, etc.). • Perform a count from the shelf to the ledger; two people should perform the count, which should be independent of the storekeeping function. • Calculate production and inventory (food); revalue them once per quarter at the minimum. Establish requirements and definitions for production items.

Proposed Internal Controls for Inventories

Controlling Inventory Count and Valuation

Control	Risk If Control Is Not in Place	Example of Method to Achieve Control Objective
		• Use standards for calculations of guestroom supplies and inventories (linens, housekeeping carts, amenities, stationery, etc.).
		• Count all circulating inventories and supplies, as applicable (e.g., bars, retail outlets, etc.).
		• Price inventory items (most recent cost; first-in, first-out; weighted moving average; etc.); apply a pricing method consistently.
		• Extend and total inventories; independently verify them.
		• Post and reconcile adjustments for accelerated physical counts.
		• Adjust perpetual records and the general ledger control to match the results of the physical count. Appropriately adjust the cost of sale.
		• Document an explanation of significant variances.

Proposed Internal Controls for Inventories

Controlling Operating Equipment

Control	Risk If Control Is Not in Place	Example of Method to Achieve Control Objective
Establish a procedure for the control of and accounting for reserve and in-use operating equipment.	• Excessive purchases or overstocking may occur. • Undetected theft or misappropriation may occur. • The amount of inventory may be insufficient to meet operating requirements. • Assets may be improperly valued. • Operating costs may be over- or understated.	• Establish appropriate requirements for reserve operating equipment. • Separate reserve (noncirculating) and in-use operating equipment. • Set up perpetual records for reserve operating equipment. • Determine valuation requirements for in-use operating equipment (i.e., the percentage of current cost applied to each category: china, glass, linen, silver). Ensure consistent application. • Make sure all items to be included are properly identified and listed. Agree upon terms and units of measure. • Set up count areas; make sure all items are organized and labeled. • Perform counts once per year at a minimum (counts may be performed cyclically or quarterly).

Proposed Internal Controls for Inventories

Controlling Operating Equipment

Control	Risk If Control Is Not in Place	Example of Method to Achieve Control Objective
		• Make sure the inventory of linen and glass in guestrooms is based on a standard room configuration, with random spot checks for verification of the standard. • Adjust in-use balances based on physical counts and appropriate valuation adjustments. • Allocate costs to appropriate operating departments. • Investigate significant shortages between count periods (for example, breakage, loss, and theft).

Food and Beverage Costs

Internal controls that effectively reduce the spoilage, waste, theft, and misappropriation of food and beverage items can increase a hotel's profits. Such controls enable accurate accounting of food and beverage costs and maximize the efficiency of food and beverage outlets.

The structure of internal controls for food and beverage costs is dependent upon the size and number of a hotel's food and beverage outlets and whether the hotel has banquet facilities. The internal control structure should address a hotel's natural cycle of food and beverage items, beginning with purchasing procedures. The physical storage, safeguarding, and requisitioning of food and beverage inventory should be integrated into the internal control structure. A hotel with banquet facilities will require an expanded control structure that includes the unique aspects of banquet costs. After the preparation and delivery of food and beverages to customers, the food and beverage costs must be accurately summarized in a timely manner and evaluated by management. Such procedures will allow reconciliations of costs through the natural cycle of food and beverage items.

Proposed Internal Controls for Food and Beverage Costs

Purchasing and Receiving

Establish purchase specifications to maintain consistency in food and beverage purchases.
Establish guidelines for determining the quantities of food and beverage purchases.
Establish procedures for the creation and maintenance of purchasing records.
Establish procedures for receiving food and beverage items.
Establish procedures for goods received without invoices, for delivery errors, and for returns.

Storing and Issuing

Establish physical controls and standards for the storage and retention of perishable and nonperishable food and beverage items.
Secure storage areas; restrict access to authorized personnel.
Establish requisition procedures.
Establish procedures for transfers from one storeroom to another, and between storerooms and food and beverage outlets.

Controlling Daily and Month-End Food and Beverage Cost Reconciliations/ Potentials and Yields

Establish procedures for monitoring and controlling daily and monthly food and beverage costs.
Establish procedures for the calculation and monitoring of food and beverage pars, standards, yields, and potentials.
Establish procedures for recording the sales values and cost equivalents for Administrative and General or Sales and Marketing food and beverage checks of officers and other employees. Include guidelines and authorization for application.

Controlling Banquets

Establish procedures to monitor banquet food-and-beverage costs.

Prepared/Submitted by: Susan J. Claremont, TCC

Proposed Internal Controls for Food and Beverage Costs

Purchasing and Receiving

Control	Risk If Control Is Not in Place	Example of Method to Achieve Control Objective
Establish purchase specifications to maintain consistency in food and beverage purchases.	• Food and beverage products may be inferior. • Waste or spoilage may increase costs. • Guests may be dissatisfied. • Revenues may decrease.	• Create written guidelines for purchase specifications and product requirements. Distribute the guidelines to purchasing and receiving personnel and F&B. • Establish bid requirements and procedures. • Perform market surveys for competitive vendor pricing.
Establish guidelines for determining the quantities of food and beverage purchases.	• Inventory may become excessive. • Costs may increase. • Waste or spoilage may occur. • Supply may be insufficient to meet demand. • Revenues may decrease.	• Set minimum and maximum inventory levels and reorder points (or par stocks). • Review forecasted restaurant covers (for perishable items). • Purchase perishable items daily. • Monitor stock levels and consumption. • Create written guidelines.

Proposed Internal Controls for Food and Beverage Costs

Purchasing and Receiving

Control	*Risk If Control Is Not in Place*	*Example of Method to Achieve Control Objective*
Establish procedures for the creation and maintenance of purchasing records.	• Some unauthorized purchases may occur. • Some unnecessary purchases may occur. • Inventory levels may become excessive. • Costs may increase. • Some items that have been paid for may not be received. • Theft or misappropriation may occur. • Waste or spoilage may occur.	• Document all food and beverage orders and submit them for appropriate F&B authorization prior to the placement of the order. • Use a multipart form for the vendor, preparer, purchasing, receiving, cost control, etc. • Obtain bids (where applicable) and document them. • Make sure the chef, head bartender, F&B director, and other appropriate personnel review and authorize the documentation as necessary. • Make sure the documents are prenumbered and sequentially accounted for. • Use standard forms and formats. • Make sure the chef orders perishables and the storekeeper orders storeroom items based on established reorder points.

Proposed Internal Controls for Food and Beverage Costs

Purchasing and Receiving

Control	Risk If Control Is Not in Place	Example of Method to Achieve Control Objective
Establish procedures for receiving food and beverage items.	• Some items that have been ordered and paid for may not be received. • Receipts may not be documented. • Costs may increase. • Theft, pilferage, or misappropriation may occur.	• Maintain an independent receiving function, segregated from purchasing and storekeeping. • Only allow items with order documents (market lists, grocery lists, beverage purchase requests, purchase orders, etc.) to be received. • Examine all invoices and packing slips, and check them against the order documents and items listed prior to accepting the items. Require the receiving clerk to stamp, date, and initial invoices and packing slips as evidence of receipt. Make sure the stamp used provides spaces for future approvals (for example, storekeeper, department head, cost control, etc.) as applicable. • Make sure the receiving clerk weighs and checks all deliveries and compares quantities and descriptions to approved order documents. (The chef may assist the clerk for specialty food items.)

Proposed Internal Controls for Food and Beverage Costs

Purchasing and Receiving

Control	Risk If Control Is Not in Place	Example of Method to Achieve Control Objective
		• Receive all F&B deliveries only at the receiving area during the posted hours of operation.
		• Periodically test and calibrate weighing scales.
		• Prepare a daily receiving report listing all invoices and packing slips for deliveries received that day. Forward the report, with the invoices and packing slips attached, to the F&B cost controller.
		• Immediately forward deliveries to the kitchen and/or storerooms, as appropriate.
		• Separate direct-issue and storeroom items.
		• If your property has an automated inventory system, prepare and print receiving documents and update inventory files where food and beverage items are received and accepted.

Proposed Internal Controls for Food and Beverage Costs

Purchasing and Receiving

Control	Risk If Control Is Not in Place	Example of Method to Achieve Control Objective

Establish procedures for goods received without invoices, for delivery errors, and for returns.	• Items may be received but not accounted for.
	• Returns may not be credited.
	• Quantities of items that have been recorded and paid for may be over- or understated.
		• Prepare multipart documents with copies for the vendor, receiver, cost control, and/or accounts payable as applicable. Forms should be prenumbered and accounted for.
		   • Use a "Goods Received without Invoice" form for all items received without an invoice.
		   • Use a "Notice of Error Correction" form to document and account for delivery errors.
		   • Use credit memos for returns.

Proposed Internal Controls for Food and Beverage Costs

Storing and Issuing

Control	Risk If Control Is Not in Place	Example of Method to Achieve Control Objective
Establish physical controls and standards for the storage and retention of perishable and nonperishable food and beverage items.	• Spoilage may occur. • Waste may occur. • Theft or pilferage may occur. • Food and beverage costs may increase. • Health hazards may increase. • Guest service may be negatively affected.	• Maintain proper storage facilities. • Control the temperatures of coolers and refrigerators. • Date stock upon receipt. • Keep storage areas clean and organized. • Rotate stock on a first-in, first-out basis. • Discard outdated stock.
Secure storage areas; restrict access to authorized personnel.	• Theft or pilferage may occur. • Some employees may gain unauthorized access to storage areas. • Some issues may be unrecorded. • Food and beverage costs may increase.	• Maintain separate food and beverage storeroom areas. • Lock all storage areas, including freezers, refrigerators, production areas, etc., and restrict access to them. • Maintain key control at the front desk or with security. • Log key issues. • Allow only authorized food and beverage personnel to hold keys. • Post storeroom hours and make sure they are adhered to.

Proposed Internal Controls for Food and Beverage Costs

Storing and Issuing

Control

Establish requisition procedures.

Risk If Control Is Not in Place

- Unauthorized transactions may occur.
- Some issues may be unauthorized.
- Food and beverage costs may increase.
- Some sales and consumption may go unrecorded.
- Theft may occur.

Example of Method to Achieve Control Objective

- Use three-part requisitions to support all food and beverage requisitions and issues. Prepare requisitions daily. Send the original to cost control and copies to the chef or bartender and the storekeeper.
- Prenumber requisitions. Maintain and log an additional numerical control at the point of issue; make sure the cost controller verifies numerical control.
- Specify items by description, unit of measure, and quantity.
- Establish beverage pars and adhere to them. Periodically verify them.
- Rule off empty spaces on requisitions to prevent unauthorized additions.
- Establish an empty-for-full-bottle exchange system.
- Use authorized full-bottle sales slips and interbar/location-transfer slips.
- Destroy empty bottles to prevent reuse.

Proposed Internal Controls for Food and Beverage Costs

Storing and Issuing

Control	Risk If Control Is Not in Place	Example of Method to Achieve Control Objective
Establish procedures for transfers from one storeroom to another, and between storerooms and food and beverage outlets.	• Unauthorized transactions may occur. • Theft or misappropriation may occur. • Pars may break down. • Some sales and consumption may go unrecorded. • Food and beverage costs may increase.	• Use unique bottle labels to identify authorized beverage issues; tightly control and secure stickers. • Cost, extend, and total requisitions daily and monthly, and compare them to actual food-and-beverage costs. Investigate and explain variances. • Make sure cost control periodically checks the completed originals against the bartender's or chef's order copy. • Use multipart, prenumbered transfer slips that are authorized and signed for. • Distribute copies to the originating storeroom or outlet, the receiving storeroom or outlet, and cost control. • Include transfers and account for them as part of the month-end cost reconciliation.

Proposed Internal Controls for Food and Beverage Costs

Controlling Daily and Month-End Food and Beverage Cost Reconciliations/ Potentials and Yields

Control

Establish procedures for monitoring and controlling daily and monthly food and beverage costs.

Risk If Control Is Not in Place

- Costs may increase.
- Losses may go unidentified or undetected.
- Transfers or adjustments may not be posted.
- Revenues may decrease.

Example of Method to Achieve Control Objective

- Calculate daily food costs and the cost of employee meals.
- Perform month-end food and beverage inventories, and calculate "issues" and food-and-beverage cost of sales based on beginning and ending inventories.
- Compare "issues" to requisition totals, and investigate significant variances.
- Verify accuracy of month-end food-and-beverage cost transfers and adjustments.

Proposed Internal Controls for Food and Beverage Costs

Controlling Daily and Month-End Food and Beverage Cost Reconciliations/ Potentials and Yields

Control	Risk If Control Is Not in Place	Example of Method to Achieve Control Objective
Establish procedures for the calculation and monitoring of food and beverage pars, standards, yields, and potentials.	• Costs may increase and revenues may decrease. • An effective measurement of performance in food preparation may not be possible. • An accurate reflection of losses in food preparation may not be possible. • Profit margins may be low or unrealistic due to poor pricing or costing. • Theft or misappropriation may go undetected. • Revenue may be lost due to sales not being rung up.	• Determine par quantity and standards as the basis for the effective evaluation of actual food costs. • Calculate the yield and compare it to actual costs. That is, cost recipes to assess the overall cost, profitability, and pricing of menu items. • Prepare and monitor food-and-beverage sales history abstracts. • Calculate beverage potentials, and identify or establish standard units of measure, cocktail abstracts, etc. Compare potentials to actual figures, and investigate significant variances. • Perform consumption tests on beverages and selected "high-food" items. • Check alcohol content (using a hydrometer) of open bottles at the bar.

Proposed Internal Controls for Food and Beverage Costs

Controlling Daily and Month-End Food and Beverage Cost Reconciliations/Potentials and Yields

Control

Establish procedures for recording the sales values and cost equivalents for Administrative and General or Sales and Marketing food and beverage checks of officers and other employees. Include guidelines and authorization for application.

Risk If Control Is Not in Place

- Food and beverage revenue and Administrative and General or Sales and Marketing costs may be overstated.
- Employees may eat unauthorized meals.
- Costs may be excessive.
- Check-signing privileges may be abused.

Example of Method to Achieve Control Objective

- Reverse revenue and write off the associated cost of revenue against the applicable operating expense account, based on the preset cost percentage. Separate percentages should be determined for food and beverages.
- Monitor usage by employees.

Proposed Internal Controls for Food and Beverage Costs

Controlling Banquets

Control	Risk If Control Is Not in Place	Example of Method to Achieve Control Objective

Establish procedures to monitor banquet food-and-beverage costs.	• Costs may increase.
	• Losses may go unidentified or undetected.
	• Transfers or adjustments may not be posted.
	• Revenues may decrease.
		• Cost menus.
		• Test consumption against banquet event orders or covers.
		• Establish a separate beverage storeroom.
		• Prepare a banquet beverage requisition and/or a consumption sheet for each function. The requisition or sheet should:
		  • Consist of three parts;
		  • Be numerically controlled;
		  • Be authorized;
		  • Have items, measurements, or quantities listed; and
		  • Be costed/extended and have totals compared to amounts/prices charged.

Personnel Administration

This section of the Control Guide consists of two main sections: Federal and State Considerations and Company Guidelines.

Complying with Federal and State Requirements

Controls must be in place to ensure that all federal and state laws are followed, in order to avoid any penalties for noncompliance. Most of the controls take the form of establishing company policy to ensure that the appropriate forms are maintained and various reports are filed on a timely basis with the correct governmental agencies.

Following Company Guidelines

Personnel administration for this area concerns a hotel's employees from the time of hire to the time of termination. During the hiring process, it is important that adequate reference checks are made in order to make the best possible hiring decisions. Fair treatment of employees is required in order to keep turnover to a minimum. This is accomplished by providing proper training along with competitive wages and benefits.

Proposed Internal Controls for Personnel Administration

Complying with Federal and State Requirements

Require new employees to complete I-9 immigration forms.
Require minors to have work permits.
Comply with minimum wage requirements.
Comply with workers' compensation laws.
Comply with Equal Employment Opportunity (EEO) requirements.
Maintain Consolidated Omnibus Budget Reconciliation Act (COBRA) insurance.

Following Company Guidelines

Require applicants to complete job application forms.
Conduct reference and background checks on candidates.
Establish fair wage guidelines.
Monitor employees' eligibility for insurance benefits.
Monitor employees' eligibility for paid vacation time.
Conduct an annual review of each employee.
Complete a termination checklist.
Conduct exit interviews.
Keep detailed employment and termination records.

Proposed Internal Controls for Personnel Administration

Complying with Federal and State Requirements

Control	Risk If Control Is Not in Place	Example of Method to Achieve Control Objective
Require new employees to complete I-9 immigration forms.	• Noncompliance with federal regulations could result in fines.	• Establish a company policy requiring all new hires to complete I-9s before starting to work.
Require minors to have work permits.	• Noncompliance with state regulations could result in fines.	• Establish a company policy requiring all minors to obtain work permits before starting to work.
Comply with minimum wage requirements.	• Noncompliance with the federal or state minimum wage could result in a wage-and-hour audit, which could cost the company back wages and a fine.	• Require the personnel director to approve all rates.
Comply with workers' compensation laws.	• The incorrect classification of employees could result in over- or underpayments of premiums.	• Require the person filing payment forms to be properly trained and the completed forms to be reviewed by accounting.
Comply with Equal Employment Opportunity (EEO) requirements.	• Noncompliance of filing could result in fines.	• Establish a company policy requiring timely filings and monitoring by an independent department, such as accounting.
Maintain Consolidated Omnibus Budget Reconciliation Act (COBRA) insurance.	• The improper handling of insurance for those no longer employed could result in fines.	• Establish a company policy to administer COBRA insurance and to include a timely follow-up with

Proposed Internal Controls for Personnel Administration

Following Company Guidelines

Control	Risk If Control Is Not in Place	Example of Method to Achieve Control Objective
Require applicants to complete job application forms.	• Management may lack adequate information to make an informed hiring decision.	• Review a candidate's application before conducting an interview, and insist that all sections of the application be completed.
Conduct reference and background checks on candidates.	• A candidate who has falsified his or her application could be hired. More time may be required to train an employee who is not qualified.	• Perform reference checks and, if appropriate for the position, conduct a background check.
Establish fair wage guidelines.	• Employees who feel the wage rate is unfair may either not work to their potential or quit.	• Conduct annual wage surveys of other hotels in the area. Stay within wage guidelines when hiring employees.
Monitor employees' eligibility for insurance benefits.	• The company may pay insurance premiums for employees who are not eligible.	• Maintain year-to-date records of hours worked and compare them to company insurance eligibility guidelines on a quarterly basis.
Monitor employees' eligibility for paid vacation time.	• The company may pay for vacation time when an employee has not earned any, or pay for more than the employee earned.	• Maintain records of total hours worked per quarter to calculate vacation hours earned. Use a vacation request form signed by management.

Proposed Internal Controls for Personnel Administration

Following Company Guidelines

Control	Risk If Control Is Not in Place	Example of Method to Achieve Control Objective
Conduct an annual review of each employee.	• The company may experience turnover if it doesn't conduct performance reviews in a timely manner.	• Department managers should be notified of employees due for annual reviews.
Complete a termination checklist.	• Employees may leave without turning in uniforms, keys, house banks, etc.	• Design a termination checklist and complete it to ensure that assets are properly returned.
Conduct exit interviews.	• The company may not find out underlying reasons for employees' departures, and unnecessary turnover may continue at a great cost to the company.	• Conduct an exit interview to determine the reasons an employee is leaving.
Keep detailed employment and termination records.	• Improper records could result in higher unemployment insurance rates.	• Document all terminations on the termination checklist or final Personnel Action Form (PAF).

Payroll

Payroll controls provide a structured, secure environment that allows your employees to accomplish a multitude of required tasks and minimize the risk of unrecognized errors and losses. The following summary of payroll controls is not meant to be all-encompassing. Instead, it provides base information a hotel can use to build and document comprehensive payroll controls and procedures specific to its organization.

Proposed Internal Controls for Payroll

Authorizing Wages, Salaries, Withholdings, and Deductions

Hire and retain employees only at rates, benefits, and perquisites determined in accordance with management's general or specific authorization.

Determine payroll withholdings and deductions based on evidence of appropriate authorization.

Preparing and Recording

Compensate company employees only at authorized rates and only for services rendered (hours worked) in accordance with management's authorization.

Correctly compute gross pay, withholdings, deductions, and net pay based on authorized rates, services rendered, and properly authorized withholding exemptions and deductions.

Correctly accumulate, classify, and summarize payroll costs and related liabilities in the appropriate accounts and periods.

Make comparisons of personnel, payroll, and work records at reasonable intervals for the timely detection and correction of errors.

Controlling Disbursements

Remit net pay and related withholdings and deductions to the appropriate employees and entities, respectively, when due.

Make disbursements only for expenditures incurred in accordance with management's authorization.

Make adjustments to cash accounts only in accordance with management's authorization.

Record disbursements at correct amounts in the appropriate period and properly classify disbursements in the accounts.

Restrict access to cash and cash disbursement records to minimize opportunities for irregular or erroneous disbursements.

Separating Functions and Physical Safeguards

Assign functions so that no single individual is in a position to both perpetrate and conceal fraud in the normal course of duties.

Limit access to personnel and payroll records to minimize opportunities for errors and irregularities.

Reconciling Banks

Make comparisons of detail records, control, accounts, and bank statements at reasonable intervals for the detection and appropriate disposition of errors or irregularities.

Proposed Internal Controls for Payroll

Authorizing Wages, Salaries, Withholdings, and Deductions

Control	Risk If Control Is Not in Place	Example of Method to Achieve Control Objective
Hire and retain employees only at rates, benefits, and perquisites determined in accordance with management's general or specific authorization.	Employees may be hired at unauthorized rates. Employees may receive unauthorized benefits and perks.	• Establish appropriate policy statements, wage and hour regulations, and union labor agreements. • Initiate and approve written personnel requisitions at designated levels of management. • Require management to approve the employee handbook or other similar documentation. • Maintain personnel files for individual employees. Include appropriate written authorizations for rates of pay, payroll deductions, and withholding exemptions.
Determine payroll withholdings and deductions based on evidence of appropriate authorization.	Improper deductions may be made.	• Obtain written authorizations from employees for all payroll deductions and withholding exemptions. • Maintain personnel files for individual employees. Include appropriate written authorizations for rates of pay, payroll deductions, and withholding exemptions.

Proposed Internal Controls for Payroll

Preparing and Recording

Control	Risk If Control Is Not in Place	Example of Method to Achieve Control Objective
Compensate company employees only at authorized rates and only for services rendered (hours worked) in accordance with management's authorization.	• Payments may be made for services not rendered.	• Require the written approval of payments by the appropriate supervisors before submitting the payments to the people preparing payroll. • Have a person whose duties are independent of personnel, payroll, processing, disbursement, and general ledger functions periodically compare pay rates per the payroll with rates per the written authorizations in the personnel files.
Correctly compute gross pay, withholdings, deductions, and net pay based on authorized rates, services rendered, and properly authorized withholding exemptions and deductions.	• Errors may go unrecognized. • Improper expenses may be incurred.	• Reconcile banquet, bellperson, and any other wage-based gratuities with those recorded on daily income statements. • Reconcile the basis for the payment of any incentive-based wages with that recorded on the financial statements. • Verify clerical operations in the preparation of payrolls by computing payroll again or reconciling payroll with independent controls (such as predetermined totals for gross pay and net pay) over source data. • Maintain time or attendance records for employees paid by the hour or by salary. • Maintain records supporting extra pay for such items as cribs, cots, etc.

Proposed Internal Controls for Payroll

Preparing and Recording

Control	Risk If Control Is Not in Place	Example of Method to Achieve Control Objective
Correctly accumulate, classify, and summarize payroll costs and related liabilities in the appropriate accounts and periods.	• Financial statements may be misstated.	• Establish a suitable chart of accounts and guidelines for determining account distributions for wages and salaries and for controlling liabilities for payroll deductions and taxes withheld. • Reconcile hours worked with the payroll statistics used for cost-accounting purposes. • Reconcile payroll cost distributions to gross pay, net pay, deductions, and withholding of gross pay.
Make comparisons of personnel, payroll, and work records at reasonable intervals for the timely detection and correction of errors.	• Unrecognized fraud may occur.	• Have a person whose duties are independent of personnel, timekeeping, payroll processing, disbursement, and general ledger functions compare data at reasonable intervals to determine gross pay.

Proposed Internal Controls for Payroll

Controlling Disbursements

Control	Risk If Control Is Not in Place	Example of Method to Achieve Control Objective
Remit net pay and related withholdings and deductions to the appropriate employees and entities, respectively, when due.	• Fines may be incurred due to nonpayment or late payment of withholdings.	• Accumulate the required information by using a tax calendar or a tickler file, instructions and tables for tax return preparation, competent tax information services, appropriate account classifications, and subsidiary records. • Maintain a timely availability of information on benefit plans and amendments, and accumulate required information by using a payment calendar or tickler file, appropriate account classifications, and subsidiary records.
Make disbursements only for expenditures incurred in accordance with management's authorization.	• Unrecognized errors or fraud may occur.	• Require responsible employees to approve payroll in writing before the issuance of payroll checks or distribution of cash for net pay. • Allow only designated employees to use and approve checks and vouchers used for all bank disbursements and transfers.

Proposed Internal Controls for Payroll

Controlling Disbursements

Control	Risk If Control Is Not in Place	Example of Method to Achieve Control Objective
Make adjustments to cash accounts only in accordance with management's authorization.	• Unrecognized errors or fraud may occur.	• Require payroll bank accounts to be under general ledger control. • Allow only designated employees to use and approve checks and vouchers for all bank disbursements and transfers.
Record disbursements at correct amounts in the appropriate period and properly classify disbursements in the accounts.	• Financial statements may be misstated.	• Balance individual disbursements with the totals to be posted to appropriate general ledger account distributions and to total disbursements to be posted to the general ledger control accounts for cash.
Restrict access to cash and cash disbursement records to minimize opportunities for irregular or erroneous disbursements.	• Unrecognized fraud may occur.	• Assign responsibility for the custody and follow-up of unclaimed wages to a responsible person who is independent of personnel, payroll processing, and cash disbursements functions. • Limit access to unissued, manual checks to designated, responsible employees who are independent of the check-signing function. • Assign responsibility for the distribution of net pay to employees who are independent of personnel, payroll preparation, timekeeping, and check preparation.

Proposed Internal Controls for Payroll

Separating Functions and Physical Safeguards

Control	Risk If Control Is Not in Place	Example of Method to Achieve Control Objective
Assign functions so that no single individual is in a position to both perpetrate and conceal fraud in the normal course of duties.	Unrecognized fraud may occur.	Provide adequate separation of responsibility for the following functions: • Written authorization of new hires, pay rates and changes thereto, benefits, changes in position, and separations; • Maintenance of personnel records; • Timekeeping; • Preparation of payrolls; • Approval of payrolls; • Cash disbursements; and • General ledger management.
Limit access to personnel and payroll records to minimize opportunities for errors and irregularities.	Distribution of confidential records may occur.	Use locking cabinets for all personnel records.

Proposed Internal Controls for Payroll

Reconciling Banks

Control	Risk If Control Is Not in Place	Example of Method to Achieve Control Objective

Make comparisons of detail records, control, accounts, and bank statements at reasonable intervals for the detection and appropriate disposition of errors or irregularities.	• Fraud and unrecognized losses may occur.	• Have an employee who is independent of payroll processing, cash disbursements, cash receipts, petty cash, and general ledger functions reconcile payroll bank accounts on a monthly basis. The procedure includes the following:
		
		  • Reconciliation of the balance per the bank to the balance per the general ledger control account and subsidiary detail records;
		
		  • Detailed comparison of deposits per the bank statement with the treasury report and the payroll subsidiary detail;
		
		  • Comparison of payees with endorsements; and
		
		  • Follow-up of reconciling items and initiation of entries to record such transactions as checks returned for insufficient funds and bank charges.
		
		• Have the employee performing the reconciliation receive bank statements and all related documentation.
		
		• Investigate and dispose of old outstanding checks on a timely

Administration

General Accounting and Financial Reporting

The general accounting function of a hotel or motel encompasses principally three basic activities: recording, classifying, and summarizing the transactions for the required books and records (and ultimately the financial reports). Managerial decision-making and regulatory and tax reporting, in addition to the daily closing of hotel transactions, necessitate accurate and timely information. The primary authoritative and instructional source for hospitality accountants is *Uniform System of Accounts for the Lodging Industry,* 9th Revised Edition, produced jointly by the Hotel Association of New York City, Inc., and the American Hotel & Motel Association. The basic objectives of a general accounting department are as follows:

1. Accounting policies and procedures are determined in accordance with management's authorization. This includes selecting an authoritative accounting principle among several valid alternatives.
2. Access to the accounting and financial records is limited to minimize opportunities for fraud and to provide reasonable protection from physical hazards.
3. Accounting entries are initiated and approved in accordance with management's authorization.
4. All accounting entries are appropriately accumulated, classified, and summarized in the accounts in accordance with *Uniform System of Accounts for the Lodging Industry,* 9th Revised Edition.

Normally, multiple levels of a hotel's staff and management perform accounting functions, depending on the size and diversity of the property's operations. Clerical and bookkeeping staffs are assigned to record and control typical tasks, such as room and beverage revenue and costs, receivables, payables, payroll, and disbursements for goods and services. Income auditors are assigned to prepare required statements of revenue and expenses, which are integrated with the work of the night audit personnel. Assistant controllers and controllers oversee the entire process and ultimately are responsible for the reporting function. The size of an accounting staff may range from a small group for mom-and-pop operations, in which the owners, employing a turnkey computerized accounting system, might complete all essential functions themselves, to large accounting staffs for properties in excess of 1,000 rooms, in which 20 to 50 people might be required to work with sophisticated, computerized back-office systems. Accounting personnel at the vice-presidential level might be present at these properties as senior financial officers.

Regardless of the size of a hotel's accounting department, the diversity of its responsibilities, or the number or types of reports produced, the accounting staff is responsible for providing service. The accounting department must work closely with operating management and other service departments to enable the hotel to meet the needs of the guests and maintain its profitability.

Hotel accounting has a foundation in Generally Accepted Accounting Principles (GAAP), promoted by the American Institute of Certified Public Accountants (AICPA). These basic principles are:

1. The Cost Principle: The transaction price is the amount to be recorded in the accounts.
2. Business Entity: The business organization maintains its own set of books separate and distinct from the owners' other interests.
3. Going Concern: This is the assumption that the business will continue indefinitely and that liquidation is not expected.
4. Unit of Measurement: Transactions recorded are based in monetary terms representing a stable unit of value. Past and present periods are to be comparable in currency used (U.S. dollars).

5. Objective Evidence: Transactions and records should reflect information that can be verified for propriety.
6. Full Disclosure: All facts pertinent to the use of the financial information as reflected in financial statements must be provided to allow interpretation and analysis by users.
7. Consistency: Once an acceptable accounting method has been adopted, it should be followed from period to period unless a change is warranted. This allows the user of the financial statements to make responsible comparisons.
8. Matching Principle: Revenues and expenses that relate to one another must be recorded in the same periods to reflect benefits and related costs.
9. Conservatism: Expenses must be recognized as soon as possible, and the recognition of revenues must be delayed until they are assured. This practice results in more reasonable (lower) income-reporting under a cautious approach.
10. Materiality: Transactions and economic events should be accounted for and recorded only if they make a difference to the user of the financial information. Accountants usually use rules of thumb, in which percentages of accounts, assets, liabilities, net income, or net worth are used to support their judgment.

Cash Basis versus Accrual Accounting

Cash and accrual bases of accounting are alternative methods of determining when to record a transaction. The cash method is a function of the actual outflow and inflow of cash as the determinant factor. The inability to match revenue and related expenses in the same period prevents this method from presenting a reasonable picture of business operations. However, this method would be appropriate if the results differed immaterially from the accrual method. The more commonly used accrual-basis accounting recognizes revenue when earned and expenses when incurred regardless of when the cash is received or disbursed. Only very small hotel properties use the cash basis method. GAAP requires the accrual method.

Fundamental Accounting Equation

The double-entry system of bookkeeping controls the relationship between a company's assets and its related liabilities and owner's equity:

$$\text{Assets} = \text{Liabilities} + \text{Owner's Equity}$$

Uniform System of Accounts for the Lodging Industry, 9th Revised Edition, provides definitions and examples of accounts and statement formats.

Assets may be defined as anything of value owned by the business. These may include, but are not limited to, cash, accounts receivable, food and beverage inventory, equipment, and investments.

Liabilities are obligations to pay money or use other assets to obtain goods and services now or in the future. These include, but are not limited to, accounts payable, loans payable, wages payable, bonds payable, and rents payable. Liabilities are the creditor's claim on assets.

Equity is the owner's claims to the assets. It represents the owner's share of the profits.

Revenue and expense accounts are defined to accumulate all transactions that have occurred during the accounting period. The result of this accumulation at year's end (or in monthly or quarterly reporting) will be reflected in the owner's equity.

The Accounting Cycle

In each accounting period of generally one year, an accounting cycle recurs, starting with the journalizing of transactions and ending with the post-closing trial balance, as follows:

1. Journalizing: analyzing, classifying, and recording transactions in a journal on a daily basis during the month.

2. Posting: copying the debits and credits of the journal entries on the ledger accounts at month-end.
3. Preparing a trial balance: summarizing the ledger accounts to prove the mathematical totals of the debits and credits. (Debits may equal credits, but the accounts can still be incorrectly posted.)
4. Posting adjusting entries: ascertaining the required adjustments to the ledger accounts and posting them to form the basis for final statements.
5. Preparing an adjusted trial balance: summarizing the adjusted trial balance accounts to ensure equality of the debits and credits.
6. Preparing the financial statements: classifying the trial balance accounts into an income statement and balance sheet.

Computerized accounting systems are offered by various vendors, with appropriate software, to perform these functions and expedite the processing with greater accuracy.

General Accounting Function

In addition to the income statement and balance sheet, the accounting department is responsible for producing numerous other reports and the performance of other tasks for management, including (but not limited to) the following:

- Daily Revenue Reports—rooms and food and beverage, by outlet
- Monthly statements of operations for each department
- Monthly budget versus actual revenue and expense comparisons
- Accounts receivable summaries—aged
- Guest and house account summarizations for complementaries
- Labor hours analysis—labor costs
- Budgeting and forecasting
- Fixed asset and equipment depreciation summaries
- Food and beverage—cost/revenue analysis
- Accounts payable summary
- Payroll analysis and approval
- Establishing controls and inventorying—china, linen, and glass
- Summarizing and reviewing travel agent commissions

Accounting is involved as an intermediary in many other functions, including:

- Reviewing and processing credit cards and other billing.
- Reviewing banquet checks for propriety and independently checking the cover count against the chef and maitre d's cover counts.
- Counting of cashier floats.
- Summarization and review of petty cash, paid outs, adjustment vouchers, and the exchange account used for disbursements.
- Supervision and review of the night audit function, in which all of the prior day's revenue, expenses, and settlements are balanced and summarized.

Organization Charts

A hotel and its accounting department should be organized for the efficient flow of information and work. Typical organization charts are shown below:

Organization Chart for a Large Lodging Establishment

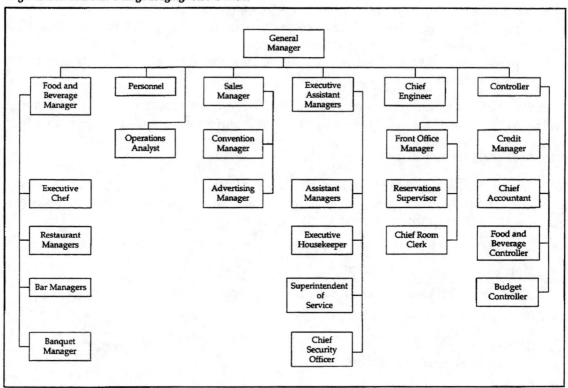

Controller's Department Organization Chart

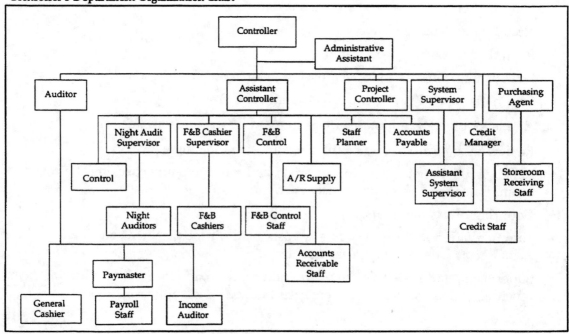

Financial Statements

Financial statements should conform to Generally Accepted Accounting Principles in form and content. The hotel's financial statements should also be separated into departmental financial statements to assist in determining the relative profitability or efficiency of all departments within the hotel. Below are samples of the hotel's financial statements.

Example Hotel Corporation
Balance Sheets
as of December 31, 19X1 and 19X0

	Date	
	19X1	19X0
Current		
Cash		
House banks		
Demand deposits		
Time deposits and certificates of deposit		
Marketable securities		
Receivables		
Accounts receivable—trade		
Notes receivable		
Other		
Total receivables		
Less allowance for doubtful accounts		
Inventories		
Prepaid expenses		
Other current assets		
Total current assets		
Investments and Advances		
Affiliates		
Others		
Property and Equipment, at cost		
Land		
Buildings		
Leasehold and leasehold improvements		
Construction in progress		
Furniture and equipment		
Less accumulated depreciation and amortization		
China, glassware, silver, linen, and uniforms		
Other Assets		
Base Stock Inventories		
Security deposits		
Cash surrender value of life insurance, net		
Deferred expenses		
Preopening expenses		
Other		
Total Assets	$	$

Example Hotel Corporation
Balance Sheets
as of December 31, 19X1 and 19X0

	Date	
	19X1	19X0

Current
  Notes Payable
  Accounts payable
  Current maturities on long-term debt
  Unearned income
  Federal and state income taxes
  Accrued liabilities
    Salaries and wages
    Interest
    Taxes—other than income
  Other current liabilities
    Total current liabilities

Long-Term Debt, less current portion

Other Noncurrent Liabilities

Deferred Income Taxes

Minority Interest

Shareholders' Equity
  Preferred stock, par value $_____
    Authorized _____ shares
    issued _____ shares
  Common stock, par value $_____
    Authorized _____ shares
    issued _____ shares
  Additional paid-in capital
  Retained earnings

  Less common stock in treasury, at cost
  _____ shares 19:_____ shares 19
    Total shareholders' equity

Commitments and Contingencies

Total Liabilities and Shareholders' Equity $_____ $_____

Example Hotel Corporation
Statement of Income and Retained Earnings
for the Years Ended December 31, 19X1 and 19X0

	Date	
	19X1	19X0
Revenues		
Rooms		
Food and beverage		
Casino		
Telephone		
Garage and parking		
Other operating revenues		
Rentals and other income		
Total		
Costs and expenses		
Rooms		
Food and beverage		
Casino		
Telephone		
Garage and parking		
Other operating costs and expenses		
Administrative and general		
Marketing		
Guest entertainment		
Property operation, maintenance, and energy costs		
Rent, property taxes, and insurance		
Interest expense		
Depreciation and amortization		
Total		
Income before gain or loss on sale of property and income taxes		
Gain or loss on sale of property		
Income taxes		
Current		
Deferred		
Net income		
Retained earnings at beginning of year		
Less dividends		
Retained earnings at end of year		
Income per common share	$_____	$_____

Example Hotel Corporation
Statement of Cash Flows
for the Years Ended December 31, 19X1 and 19X0

Cash flows from operating activities:
    Net income
    Adjustments to reconcile net income to net cash
        provided by operating activities:
    Depreciation and amortization
    Provision for losses on accounts receivable
    Gain on sale of facility
    Undistributed earnings of affiliate
    Payment received on installment note receivable
        for sale of inventory
    Change in assets and liabilities net of effects
        from purchase of Company S:
        Increase in accounts receivable
        Decrease in inventory
        Increase in prepaid expenses
        Decrease in accounts payable and accrued expenses
Increase in interest and income taxes payable
Increase in deferred taxes
Increase in other liabilities

    Total adjustments
    Net cash provided by operating activities

Cash flows from investing activities:
    Proceeds from sale of facility
    Payment received on note for sale of plant
    Capital expenditures
    Payment for purchase of Company S, net of cash
        acquired
            Net cash used in investing activities

Cash flows from financing activities:
    Net borrowing under line-of-credit agreement
    Principal payments under capital lease obligation
    Proceeds from issuance of long-term debt
    Proceeds from issuance of common stock
    Dividends paid
        Net cash provided by financing activities

Increase in cash and cash equivalents

Cash and cash equivalents at beginning of year

Cash and cash equivalents at end of year

Supplemental disclosures of cash flow information

Cash paid during the year for:
    Interest (net of amount capitalized)
    Income taxes

Supplemental schedule of noncash investing and
    financing activities:

The company purchases all of the capital stock of
    company S for $950. In conjunction with the
    acquisition, liabilities were assumed as follows:

        Par value of assets acquired
        Cash paid for capital stock

        Liabilities assumed

Example Hotel Corporation
Manager's Daily Report

Date _____

Day _____

Weather _____

NCR Closing Reset Reading NCR Opening Reset Reading Total Resets		Day		Month to Date	
		This Year	Last Year	This Year	Last Year
ROOMS	Guest				
	Public				
	Total Rooms				
FOOD	Dining Room				
	Coffee Shop				
	Specialty Room				
	Room Service				
	Functions				
	Total Food				
BEVERAGE	Dining Room				
	Coffee Shop				
	Pub				
	Specialty Room				
	Pool				
	Room Service				
	Functions				
	Total Beverage				
TELEPHONE	Local				
	Long Distance				
	Service Charges				
	Total Telephone				
RENTALS AND OTHER INCOME					
	Store Rentals				
	Newsstand, Laundry, & Valet				
	Commissions				
	Vending Machines				
	Checkrooms				
	Golf				
	Miscellaneous				
	Total Rental and Other Income				
TOTAL SALES					
SALES TAX					
ROOMS TAX					
GRATUITIES—BANQUET					
GRATUITIES—PAID OUT					
FRONT OFFICE—PAID OUT					
	Cash Sales (to Cash, Page 2)				
	Charge Sales (to A/R, Page 2)				
	TOTAL INCOME				

General Areas of Concern for an Internal Hotel Audit

An internal auditor should consider the following areas when designing a hotel audit plan.

Cash—House Banks

A hotel usually maintains separate house banks for each cashier and his or her corresponding revenue center. Cashiers are responsible for collecting the revenue for their particular revenue centers. They may be receiving cash, checks, credit card vouchers, or other forms of payment. The cashier's bank and receipts are deposited daily in a special safe. Audit work in this area should be coordinated with the night audit review and includes, but is not limited to, obtaining a listing of all house banks, counting cash on hand in the presence of the respective custodian, obtaining confirmation from custodians whose cash was not counted, and agreeing all house banks to the general ledger control account.

Inventories

Hotel inventories are generally classified as merchandise and supplies. Merchandise represents assets sold to customers, such as food and liquor. Inventories of merchandise are accounted for using either the periodic or the perpetual method. Supplies represent assets used in the normal course of operations.

Inventories of supplies, particularly linen, glassware, and silver, are accounted for using one of three methods:

1. Capitalization of initial investment and expense of all replacements.
2. Capitalization of initial investment and expense of all replacements. Annual adjustment to actual physical count.
3. Capitalization of initial investment and depreciation over a relatively short period of time. Capitalization of all replacements and corresponding depreciation. Annual adjustment to actual physical count.

Due Bills

It has been customary for hotels to enter into contracts with the media in order to exchange hotel services in return for advertising. Although less common today, there is some indication that the practice is still followed. The advertising is exchanged for complimentary rooms and in some cases complimentary meals. Such agreements are usually called Trade Advertising Agreements or Exchange Due Bills.

Whenever such an agreement is made, it should be evidenced in a written contract that sets forth the exact terms of exchange and that is signed by both parties. Trade advertising agreements usually expire after a given period of time. The effective period of time should, of course, be specified in the text of the written contract. Care must be taken in this respect to ensure that the hotel is able to take advantage of the entire amount of the consideration to which it is entitled. Before entering into such an agreement, management should make sure the hotel will be able to use the advertising for which the commitment is being made.

In accordance with *Uniform System of Accounts for the Lodging Industry*, 9th Revised Edition, the expense of advertising paid for by such contracts should be charged to the marketing department's "Advertising-Exchange (due bills)" at the value of the services provided by the hotel. Memo entries could be maintained for the value of unused advertising, but it is preferable to record the cost or value of the advertising program as an asset and to set up a corresponding liability account for the value of the services to be rendered by the hotel.

Payroll

Wages are a hotel's single largest expense, comprising as much as 60 percent of all expenditures, depending on the type of hotel and the services it performs.

In other industries, gross pay is equal to either the fixed wage rate or the number of hours worked times the hourly rate. However, in a hotel there are many people who receive compensation in the form of tips and/or free room and board. Where this situation exists, an employee's gross pay is calculated as follows:

> Gross wages
> − Tips
> _____
> = Taxable wages for federal and state withholding tax purposes
>
> − Value of room and board
> _____
> = Taxable wages for Social Security tax purposes

Some hotels do not provide free room and board, but rather charge the employees for meals and lodging. The computation of gross pay in this case is somewhat different.

> Gross wages
> − Tips
> _____
> = Taxable wages for Social Security tax purposes
>
> − Value of room and board
> _____
> = Taxable wages for federal and state withholding tax purposes

Tips. All employees who receive tips must declare them as part of their salary. The hotel will issue to each employee a form for declaring such tips, and the employee must return the form to the accounting department for inclusion in the pay records. Except for tips charged on a guest bill, the hotel cannot maintain records of the tips received by each employee, nor is it the responsibility of the hotel to determine whether the employee is declaring the full amount of the tips actually received, unless the hotel has knowledge that would contradict the employee's declaration.

Receivables and Revenue

Hotels are usually complex organizations that offer a multitude of services. While the provision of rooms is generally the principle business, restaurants, bars, telephone services, etc., can comprise a significant source of revenue for the operation. These ancillary services are generally provided at some additional charge, and guests of the hotel normally have the privilege of adding the charge for these services to their daily bill.

Revenues are controlled for each ancillary service on an individual basis, with each department responsible for generating records of all guest and nonguest activity. In order to maintain an accurate listing of accounts receivable, a hotel must keep a list of all guests and others with charge privileges and process all of the ancillary department charges on a daily basis. This is usually done at the front office, since all guest registration and credit information is close at hand. Through the use of computers, this activity is becoming more automated, and in the future, hotels will probably rely even less on mechanical equipment and more on computers.

The general flow of work requires the preparation of a daily departmental summary of information for the accounting department so that the general ledger may be updated. Following this methodology, there should be sufficient information for a proper accounting entry for each sale and enough detail provided so that the hotel can maintain a listing of accounts receivable by individual guests. This is outlined in the flow chart form on the next page.

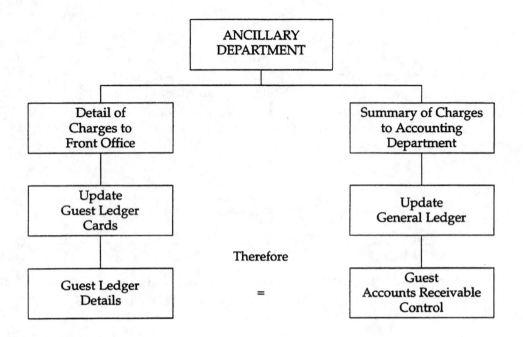

The Night Audit

Throughout the day, various transactions are recorded at the front desk. Guests check in; patronize the restaurants, bars, newsstand, barber shop, etc.; and charge these services and products to their guest accounts receivable.

In order to be assured that all of this income has been recorded, a night audit is performed every day, seven days a week, usually between the hours of midnight and 8 AM. The person performing this function is appropriately called a night auditor. The basic functions of the night audit are:

1. Recording and control of room sales,
2. Reconciling and providing all charge sales and payments posted by the desk clerks to the individual guest folios, and
3. Reconciliation and proof of accounts receivable balances each day.

The manual night audit, completed using a "hand transcript," summarizes sales by department and credits by type from the individual guest folios. These department totals are then balanced to the totals of the individual department vouchers. Then, after all the departments are in balance, the transcript sheets are balanced using the following basic formula:

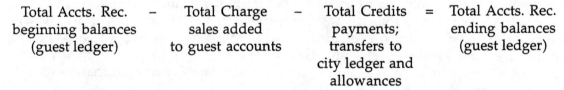

This manual system can be extremely time-consuming, and for this reason it is seldom found today, except in very small motels and hotels.

With machine-based systems, there is no need to summarize the transactions by department, since the machine maintains running departmental totals as the vouchers are posted during the day. The night auditor, when coming on duty, takes a trial balance (reading) of these departmental totals on a "D" card. The individual department vouchers are then totaled and must equal the machine total. For example, an adding machine tape total of the restaurant checks should equal the machine "Food" total.

At this point, the night auditor places the machine into the "Trial Balance" position, if the machine provides for this option. The Trial Balance option accumulates the ending balance from each guest folio as the room charges are posted.

The night auditor then posts the room charges and applicable tax for each room. The night auditor takes the machine out of Trial Balance and takes a Trial Balance (reading) of all the departments' credits. Finally, the night auditor obtains total debts and total credits per the Trial Balance by putting the machine in Trial Balance and pressing the "Debit Balance" and "Credit" keys. The rooms income per this Trial Balance must agree with the total of the room count sheet prepared by the night desk clerk. The net of the transfers (total credits less total debits) should equal the manually prepared tape of the balances on the folios being transferred to the city ledger.

The night auditor must then prove the balance in accounts receivable. The ending balance of the guests' accounts receivable from the previous night is carried forward to this night's "D" card. The total debits are added to this balance, and then the total credits are subtracted. The result should be the ending balance in the accounts receivable. This figure can be proved by subtracting the total credits per the Trial Balance key reading from the total debits per the Trial Balance key reading.

Once the night audit is in balance, a new "D" card is prepared using a clear key. The audit tape is then removed from the machine, the date is changed, and a reading is taken to show on the next day's audit tape that all the departments are zero balanced. The detailed vouchers, paid folios, "D" cards, etc., are then placed together for review by the accounting department.

Night Audit Procedure (Manual)

Registered Guests (Guest Ledger)
Step

1. Beginning balance is last night's ending balance
2. Room rates posted to folios
3. Folios totaled
4. Folios posted to transcript—includes all guest charges for the day
5. Transcript footed and crossfooted
6. Guest restaurant checks totaled—must equal the transcript food total
7. Same for beverage checks
8. Same for telephone vouchers
9. Same for other ancillary service departments
10. Same for paid outs and allowance vouchers
11. Room income must agree with the "Night Desk Clerk Revenue Report"
12. Total cash column must equal the total of cash sheets and the total of folios being charged to the city ledger
13. Total "transfers" must equal the actual folios being charged to the city ledger
14. Ending balance of transcript must equal the total of guest folios of guests still in the "house"

Nonregistered Guests (City Ledger)
Step

1. City ledger sheet is totaled
2. Restaurant checks are totaled and must equal total food on city ledger sheet
3. Same for bar checks, etc.

Retention Requirements for Hotels

Listed below are suggested record-retention guidelines. However, consider that tax waivers may have been issued, and hold the records accordingly.

1. Journals and Ledgers
    a. General Ledger
    b. General Journal
    c. Cash Receipts Journal
    d. Cash Disbursement Journal
    e. Sales Journal
    f. Discount and Allowance Journal
    g. Voucher Register

    These should be accessible to the accounting office for five years and then placed in permanent storage.

2. Subsidiary Ledger

    This is an accounts receivable ledger. It may be destroyed three years after the accounts are paid. It should be accessible to the accounting office for one year and held in storage for two years.

3. Vouchers and Invoices

    a. Purchase Voucher

        (1) Fixed assets, additions, replacements, and permanent records should be filed separately from other vouchers and be kept accessible to the accounting office for at least two years. They then should be placed in permanent storage.

        (2) Other purchase vouchers should be accessible to the accounting office for one year, kept in storage for six years, and then destroyed.

    b. Restaurant Checks and Other Cash Vouchers

        Charge restaurant checks should be retained until the tax audit is complete or at least four years, unless shorter periods are granted by law. They then may be destroyed.

4. Payroll Records

    a. Employment Applications
        These should be kept for three years after an employee leaves.

    b. Employment Contract
        These are permanent records.

    c. Time Cards and Time Books
        These may be destroyed after eight years.

5. Miscellaneous Account Records

    a. Bank Statements and Cancelled Checks
        Destroy them after eight years.

    b. Storeroom Requisitions
        Retain them until the regular audit is completed (at least one year).

   c. Cash Transmittal Envelopes
      Destroy them after one year.

6. Insurance Records

   a. Insurance Policies
      Retain these for five years after the expiration of the policies. They then may be destroyed.

   b. Accident and Fire Inspection Reports
      Destroy these after eight years.

   c. Safety Reports and Disability Reports
      Destroy these after eight years.

   d. Claims
      Retain these for ten years after a settlement. They then may be destroyed.

7. Licenses and Sales Tax Correspondence on Sales and Purchases

   Destroy them after six years.

8. Permanent Corporate Records

   a. Bylaws and the charter of incorporation and amendments thereto
   b. Legal documents in connection with mergers, consolidations, reorganizations, and similar actions that affect the identity or organization of the company
   c. Minutes of meetings of stockholders and directors
   d. Minutes of meetings of executive and other directors' committees
   e. Detailed capital stock journals, ledgers, or their equivalents
   f. Bond indentures, underwriting, mortgage, and other long-credit agreements
   g. All other bond records or their equivalents
   h. Contracts and agreements
   i. Tax returns and other tax records
   j. Certified financial statements and other certifications and reports of all examinations and audits conducted by public and certified public accountants

Proposed Internal Controls for Financial Reporting

Ensuring the Accuracy and Completeness of the Financial Data Provided to Various Parties

Authorize accounting principles.
Authorize entries and adjustments.
Authorize the issuance of specific financial statements.
Prepare general journal entries.
Summarize general ledger balances.
Combine departmental information accurately.
Prepare appropriate disclosures.
Protect records from hazards and misuse.

Proposed Internal Controls for Financial Reporting

Ensuring the Accuracy and Completeness of the Financial Data Provided to Various Parties

Control	Risk If Control Is Not in Place	Example of Method to Achieve Control Objective
Authorize accounting principles.	• The hotel's financial information may be unreliable or inconsistent.	• Use accounting manuals and policy manuals containing the accounting practices the hotel should follow. Use *Uniform System of Accounts for the Lodging Industry*, 9th Revised Edition. • Assign responsibility for the approval of the accounting principles used. • Assign responsibility for the appropriate review and approval of significant estimates or judgments used in preparing financial information.
Authorize entries and adjustments.	• The hotel's financial information may be inaccurate.	• Assign responsibility for the preparation and approval of journal entries. • Require approval for adjusting journal entries.
Authorize the issuance of specific financial statements.	• The credibility of the business may be damaged.	• Assign responsibility for the preparation and review of financial statements and other financial reports.

Proposed Internal Controls for Financial Reporting

Ensuring the Accuracy and Completeness of the Financial Data Provided to Various Parties

Control	Risk If Control Is Not in Place	Example of Method to Achieve Control Objective
Prepare general journal entries.	• The hotel's financial information may be inaccurate.	• Use a chart of accounts and an accounting procedures manual containing adequate details and clear instructions. • Institute procedures for the preparation of journal entries, including required documentation. • Require the use and accountability of prenumbered journal entry forms. • Use standard journal entries. • Require a period-to-period comparison of recurring journal entries.

Proposed Internal Controls for Financial Reporting

Ensuring the Accuracy and Completeness of the Financial Data Provided to Various Parties

Control	Risk If Control Is Not in Place	Example of Method to Achieve Control Objective
Summarize general ledger balances.	• The hotel's financial information may be inaccurate.	• Assign responsibility for the review of general ledger balances, including an agreement with underlying records (for example, subsidiary ledgers and workpaper account analyses). • Institute procedures for reflecting necessary general-ledger corrections and adjustments on a timely basis (for example, the preparation of the preliminary general ledger that is reviewed prior to the preparation of the final general ledger for the period). • Require an analytical review of general ledger balances. • Require closing schedules for periodic general-ledger closings.
Combine departmental information accurately.	• The hotel's financial information may be inaccurate.	• Institute procedures for obtaining financial statements from reporting units (for example, reporting forms containing data necessary for the preparation of consolidated financial statements or other financial reports). • Require closing schedules for reporting units.

Proposed Internal Controls for Financial Reporting

Ensuring the Accuracy and Completeness of the Financial Data Provided to Various Parties

Control	*Risk If Control Is Not in Place*	*Example of Method to Achieve Control Objective*
Prepare appropriate disclosures.	• The hotel's credibility may be damaged due to the inappropriate preparation of data.	• Assign responsibility for the final review and approval of financial statements. • Assign the responsibility for the establishment of procedures for accumulating information disclosed with financial statements (for example, notes to financial statements), including the review of such information. • Require an analytical review of financial statements.
Protect records from hazards and misuse.	• The hotel may be exposed to loss from common hazards.	• Keep important records in storage facilities that are locked or under continuous surveillance. • Restrict office access to authorized personnel by locking facilities. • Protect records against physical hazards (for example, use fireproof cabinets).

Loss Prevention and Risk Management

Loss prevention starts with a hotel's owners and extends through management to employees at every level. Planning, the education of employees, and ongoing evaluation are critical components of the following controls, which are designed to reduce the risks inherent in the operation of a hotel.

Proposed Internal Controls for Loss Prevention and Risk Management

Keeping Guests and Employees Safe

Promote safety awareness.
Fill out incident reports accurately and submit them on a timely basis.

Restricting Access to the Property

Protect the perimeter.
Designate an employee entrance and exit.
Restrict access to interior areas.

Protecting the Guestroom

Establish physical security in guestrooms.
Inform guests of guestroom safety features.

Controlling Keys

Issue keys only to employees requiring access.
Document key issuance.
Rekey locks.

Protecting against Fires and Planning for Emergencies

Educate all employees in fire prevention and safety.
Maintain adequate fire protection equipment.
Institute an emergency response and evacuation plan.

Evaluating the Loss Prevention Program

Establish a protection committee.
Perform periodic safety audits.

Reducing Internal Theft

Verify applicant information.

Limiting Property Liability and Loss

Provide safe-deposit-box protection.
Obtain cost-effective insurance coverage.
Assign insurance coordination responsibilities to a qualified individual.

Proposed Internal Controls for Loss Prevention and Risk Management

Keeping Guests and Employees Safe

Control	Risk If Control Is Not in Place	Example of Method to Achieve Control Objective
Promote safety awareness.	• Guest and employee injuries could result in medical and worker compensation costs, lost productivity, and litigation.	• Make sure employees are alert for unsafe property conditions (for example, hazardous chemicals and equipment) and aware of proper working conditions (that is, the use of safety devices and the proper operation of equipment). Establish an employee training program to increase awareness of proper working conditions.
Fill out incident reports accurately and submit them on a timely basis.	• The hotel may violate federal or state requirements, fail to correct an unsafe condition or procedure, and respond with inadequate information in the event of litigation.	• Assign the responsibility for incident reporting to a responsible individual, and periodically review completed reports.

Proposed Internal Controls for Loss Prevention and Risk Management

Restricting Access to the Property

Control	Risk If Control Is Not in Place	Example of Method to Achieve Control Objective
Protect the perimeter.	• Unauthorized individuals may gain access to the hotel; employee and guest safety may be threatened; and facility or guest property may be damaged.	• Install locks on exterior doors that provide access to guest and employee areas and equipment storage. Install adequate lighting around the perimeter and in guest and employee areas.
Designate an employee entrance and exit.	• Employee theft and unauthorized access to employee areas may occur.	• Monitor employee entry and access for the removal of items from the property, and require the use of a pass.
Restrict access to interior areas.	• Unauthorized individuals may gain access to the hotel; employee and guest safety may be threatened; and facility or guest property may be damaged.	• Establish an employee training program to inform employees of access controls and procedures for reporting unauthorized individuals to the appropriate personnel.

Proposed Internal Controls for Loss Prevention and Risk Management

Protecting the Guestroom

Control	Risk If Control Is Not in Place	Example of Method to Achieve Control Objective
Establish physical security in guestrooms.	• Guest safety may be threatened and the loss of guest property may occur.	• Install door locks, safety chains, and door viewers.
Inform guests of guestroom safety features.	• Guest safety may be threatened and the loss of guest property may occur.	• Place tent cards informing guests of safety features (such as the door viewer) in the guestrooms.

Proposed Internal Controls for Loss Prevention and Risk Management

Controlling Keys

Control	Risk If Control Is Not in Place	Example of Method to Achieve Control Objective
Issue keys only to employees requiring access.	• Unauthorized individuals may gain access to restricted areas of the property (including guestrooms).	• Issue keys to employees based upon their need and the appropriateness to their position.
Document key issuance.	• Individuals no longer employed by the property may gain access to keys, and the property may fail to document a reasonable assurance with respect to key control.	• Have a responsible management employee start and maintain a control log for the keys issued (including areas for the date, issuing employee, key description, and employee signature).
Rekey locks.	• Unauthorized individuals may gain access to restricted areas of the property and the property may fail to provide a reasonable assurance with respect to guest safety.	• Establish procedures for a periodic or phased rekeying of all locks (especially guestroom locks).

Proposed Internal Controls for Loss Prevention and Risk Management

Protecting Against Fires and Planning for Emergencies

Control	Risk If Control Is Not in Place	Example of Method to Achieve Control Objective
Educate all employees in fire prevention and safety.	• Injury, loss of life, and property damage may occur.	• Require the presentation of fire safety procedures and regulations to all employees on a periodic basis by fire officials (the documentation of the training should be prepared and maintained by management).
Maintain adequate fire protection equipment.	• Injury, loss of life, and property damage may occur. The hotel may fail to comply with federal and state requirements.	• Establish procedures for the periodic testing of fire protection equipment (such as smoke alarms, sprinklers, and fire extinguishers) and document the test results.
Institute an emergency response and evacuation plan.	• The failure to respond to hazardous conditions may result in injury, the loss of life, or additional property damage. The hotel may fail to comply with federal and state requirements.	• Develop an emergency response and evacuation plan and assign responsibility for the implementation of the plan to a responsible management employee.

Proposed Internal Controls for Loss Prevention and Risk Management

Evaluating the Loss Prevention Program

Control	Risk If Control Is Not in Place	Example of Method to Achieve Control Objective
Establish a protection committee.	• The hotel may fail to coordinate all aspects of the loss prevention program and identify areas requiring attention.	• Establish a protection committee that would meet periodically to systematically review incident reports, training programs, and the results of safety inspections.
Perform periodic safety audits.	• The hotel may fail to identify unsafe conditions and areas of noncompliance with federal and state requirements.	• Assign a responsible individual to perform physical inspections, determine compliance with established safety procedures, and report the results to management.

Proposed Internal Controls for Loss Prevention and Risk Management

Reducing Internal Theft

Control	Risk If Control Is Not in Place	Example of Method to Achieve Control Objective
Verify applicant information.	• The hotel may hire individuals who represent a high risk of internal theft.	• Establish procedures for the verification of applicant information, within legal constraints, by a responsible individual (such as an employee or agent) prior to extending an offer of employment to a candidate.

Proposed Internal Controls for Loss Prevention and Risk Management

Limiting Property Liability and Loss

Control	Risk If Control Is Not in Place	Example of Method to Achieve Control Objective
Provide safe-deposit-box protection.	• The hotel may be liable for guest losses because of a lack of reasonable assurance.	• Require the guest to complete a form at the time of deposit (including an agreement of acceptance, an access record, and a waiver), and restrict access to the area where the boxes are located.
Obtain cost-effective insurance coverage.	• The hotel may experience a loss resulting from crime, property damage, litigation, or a business interruption.	• Evaluate the risk of a loss from harmful events and obtain insurance coverage commensurate with the acceptable risk, given cost considerations.
Assign insurance coordination responsibilities to a qualified individual.	• The hotel may fail to understand elements of insurance coverage (especially limitations and exclusions) and may not comply with procedures for reporting incidents.	• Select a qualified individual (such as an employee or agent) to be the risk manager.

Computer Systems

The accounting systems of a hotel may be small and simple or massive and complex. Hotels generally require systems capable of processing large numbers of various types of transactions. Sophisticated computer systems, including point-of-sale registers, may be used to process these transactions. Such systems are designed and installed not only to produce the general ledger balances from which financial statements are prepared, but also to produce management and operating information.

A hotel's use of Electronic Data Processing (EDP) has a potentially significant impact on its internal control system, because EDP is used to process transactions, maintain data files, and prepare trial balances or other accounting analyses that significantly affect the accounts of a hotel. A hotel's computer system also may adversely affect its internal audit; transactions processing may be too complex or the volume of data too great to allow the hotel to independently verify the accuracy or completeness of processing.

The use of EDP to perform significant and complex processing of financial transactions and to prepare financial information for internal and external reporting entails risks. Such risks include:

- The loss of transaction trials in automation
- The lack of adequate system documentation
- Unauthorized access to files
- The lack of a separation of duties
- Inadequate maintenance and recovery procedures

The following pages explain internal controls that will help mitigate or reduce the risks involved in using a complex EDP system.

Proposed Internal Controls for Computer Systems

Control access to computer systems and applications.

Protect sensitive company information from accidental or intentional misuse or disclosure.

Establish a security administration function for each major system.

Include security awareness training in the employees' training program.

Establish an appropriate environment for the equipment in the computer room.

Purchase sufficient insurance coverage for all computer assets.

Cover all major hardware with preventative maintenance contracts, and arrange for the use of backup equipment in an emergency.

Ensure the reliable installation, maintenance, and physical security of all telecommunications.

Make sure all acquisitions of software and hardware are fully justified, approved, and compatible with the existing environment.

Implement controls over all software and hardware changes.

Make sure computer systems are used effectively and for their intended purposes.

Proposed Internal Controls for Computer Systems

Control	Risk If Control Is Not in Place	Example of Method to Achieve Control Objective
Control access to computer systems and applications.	• Uncontrolled access could lead to unauthorized or fraudulent changes.	• Require employees to follow the principle of least privilege (that is, access should be allowed only for the entry of functions required to perform day-to-day duties). • Restrict access to sensitive functions. • Require employees to change their passwords regularly. • Determine who has the authority to approve access. • Document current access levels for each user.
Protect sensitive company information from accidental or intentional misuse or disclosure.	• The company could experience financial loss or public embarrassment. • The company's competitors could gain an advantage.	• Require users to log off when leaving terminals unattended. • Keep all sensitive reports and documents in a secure location. • Dispose of all sensitive documents in a secure manner. • Store all diskettes containing sensitive information in a secure location. • Do not store sensitive information on PC hard drives unless the PCs are located in secure areas or the on-off switches have locks on them.

Proposed Internal Controls for Computer Systems

Control	Risk If Control Is Not in Place	Example of Method to Achieve Control Objective
Establish a security administration function for each major system.	• Security may become difficult to control and coordinate. Violations may not be adequately detected or investigated.	• Assign security administration responsibility to a specific individual or group. • Make sure the position of security administrator is independent of the system being administered. • Perform routine monitoring, including a review of security violation logs. • Establish written security administration procedures, including details of the level of access for various job functions. • Establish procedures to ensure that security access cards and similar materials are collected from terminated employees before they leave.

Proposed Internal Controls for Computer Systems

Control	Risk If Control Is Not in Place	Example of Method to Achieve Control Objective
Include security awareness training in the employees' training program.	• The security policy may not be satisfactorily carried out, leaving the company open to security violations.	• Require senior management to document and approve the security policy. • Do not allow the use of unauthorized software. • Consider putting in place sanctions against employees who violate the security policy. • Make new employees aware of the security policy during induction training. • Make sure security awareness training is an ongoing process.
Establish an appropriate environment for the equipment in the computer room.	• Computer performance may deteriorate or break down, and processing errors may occur.	• Restrict access to the computer area to authorized individuals only. • Locate computers away from potential hazards as much as possible. • Make sure fire alarms, smoke detectors, fire extinguishers, and similar equipment is regularly tested and maintained in good working order. • Keep the area in and around the computer room neat to reduce the risk of fire.

Proposed Internal Controls for Computer Systems

Control	Risk If Control Is Not in Place	Example of Method to Achieve Control Objective
Purchase sufficient insurance coverage for all computer assets.	• An accident could cause extensive losses for the company.	• Maintain a listing of all computer equipment and serial numbers. • Make sure insurance is provided under a general business policy or a special computer policy for all hardware and software.
Cover all major hardware with preventative maintenance contracts, and arrange for the use of backup equipment in an emergency.	• Equipment failure could result in the disruption of business and possibly its failure.	• Make sure critical applications are backed up on appropriate equipment. • Make sure major equipment is covered by a preventative maintenance program.
Ensure the reliable installation, maintenance, and physical security of all telecommunications.	• Disruption of the telecommunications links could disrupt the whole computing service.	• Perform a cost-benefit analysis before the acquisition of any telecommunications equipment. • Consider potential or required hardware or software interfaces with other applications/systems before making any decision to purchase telecommunications equipment. • Maintain a complete and up-to-date telecommunications network diagram. • Implement adequate security controls over dial-in lines. • Purchase equipment only from reputable vendors.

Proposed Internal Controls for Computer Systems

Control

Make sure all acquisitions of software and hardware are fully justified, approved, and compatible with the existing environment.

Risk If Control Is Not in Place

- Uncontrolled hardware and software purchases could waste money and jeopardize system integrity.

Example of Method to Achieve Control Objective

- Require a cost-benefit analysis to be carried out before each acquisition.
- Fully consider possible incompatibility problems before any acquisition.
- Make sure all acquisitions are fully authorized and in accordance with company policy.
- Use only sealed copies of software from reputable vendors, to avoid the risk of viruses.
- Hold licenses for all software.
- Do not allow the use of unauthorized software on office computers.
- Add all new acquisitions to the maintenance agreements and insurance policies as necessary.

Proposed Internal Controls for Computer Systems

Control

Implement controls over all software and hardware changes.

Risk If Control Is Not in Place

- Unauthorized or inconsistent changes could be made, jeopardizing the integrity of the application data.

Example of Method to Achieve Control Objective

- Require all changes to be authorized in writing.
- Fully test all changes before implementation.
- Establish provisions for undoing a change in cases where the change does not work.
- Make sure procedures for making emergency changes are available when normal authorization procedures cannot be followed.
- Add all hardware changes to the hardware documentation as they occur.
- Maintain a transaction trail for all software changes, showing who made each change, when the change was made, and on what authority it was made.

Proposed Internal Controls for Computer Systems

Control	Risk If Control Is Not in Place	Example of Method to Achieve Control Objective
Make sure computer systems are used effectively and for their intended purposes.	• Hardware may be used for purposes that are not justified on cost-benefit grounds.	• Make sure systems are used for purposes for which they have been authorized. • Make maximum use of system features and capabilities. • Print only necessary reports, and make a list of all potential reports available to the systems' users. • Make sure all report names, codes, and abbreviations are meaningful. • Review all available system activity logs to identify any unauthorized activity. • Put in place a regular program of system housekeeping, including archiving procedures. • Monitor system performance regularly to ensure that system faults are captured and rectified at the earliest possible time.

Administration

Proposed Internal Controls for Administration

Controlling Annual Forecasts

Forecast revenue for each revenue center by month, based on forecasted occupancy.
Forecast expenses based on the occupancy volumes used to generate revenues.
Review and compare monthly forecasts of revenues and expenses.

Controlling Capital Expenditures

Obtain, in writing, all approvals necessary to proceed with projects.
Prepare forms necessary for the initiation of projects: purchase orders, major expense
   forms, contracts, etc.
Document any change of the original project, purchase order, or contract.
Ensure the proper payments for planned projects.
Compare the budget to actual expenditures and planned expenditures.
Prepare an overview of capital expenditures made in the previous seven years.
Prepare a list of all projects that may be desired or needed.
Prepare the funding amounts to be spent on projects.
Prioritize the project listing by importance to the ongoing operation and the objectives of
   management.

Proposed Internal Controls for Administration

Controlling Annual Forecasts

Control	Risk If Control Is Not in Place	Example of Method to Achieve Control Objective
Forecast revenue for each revenue center by month, based on forecasted occupancy.	• The hotel may be unable to evaluate the accuracy of its revenue achievement assumptions.	• For each day of the year, forecast occupancy based on current and historical information. Multiply the projected revenue per volume unit to determine revenue by day, month, and year.
Forecast expenses based on the occupancy volumes used to generate revenues.	• Expense items may not be achievable based on projected revenues.	• For each unit of occupancy volume, determine the appropriate related cost to produce the volume. Fixed-cost items should be listed at a fixed cost.
Review and compare monthly forecasts of revenues and expenses.	• A drop in revenue or an increase in expenses may require a change in operational plans in order to achieve the required targets.	• For each line item, review the forecast and determine the steps necessary to recapture the projected financial results.

Proposed Internal Controls for Administration

Controlling Capital Expenditures

Control	Risk If Control Is Not in Place	Example of Method to Achieve Control Objective
Obtain, in writing, all approvals necessary to proceed with projects.	• Approval of projects may be denied in the future.	• Require the submission of planned expenditures to the proper authorities to obtain approval.
Prepare forms necessary for the initiation of projects: purchase orders, major expense forms, contracts, etc.	• Quoted prices may vary if they are not in writing prior to the initiation of the project.	• Prepare a document that details the work that needs to be done and the items that need to be paid for, including fees, taxes, and delivery charges.
Document any change of the original project, purchase orders, or contract.	• The vendor may include charges that were not agreed to in the original document.	• Prepare a document that details any changes to a project, and have the document signed by authorized people.
Ensure the proper payments for planned projects.	• The vendor may prepare an invoice prior to the completion of the work, or the vendor may include nonauthorized charges.	• Compare the invoiced amount to the quoted price prior to the payment of the invoice. Require a management representative to compare a detail of the project to the invoiced work and to physically review and approve a payment.
Compare the budget to actual expenditures.	• The budget may be exceeded in certain areas, eliminating the funds for other projects.	• Compare the budgeted amounts listed for each project to line item expenditures.

Proposed Internal Controls for Administration

Controlling Capital Expenditures

Control	Risk If Control Is Not in Place	Example of Method to Achieve Control Objective
Prepare an overview of capital expenditures made in the previous seven years.	• Projects that have been completed recently may be redone, or they may not be fully amortized, causing an early reduction of assets.	• List all major projects done in the previous seven years and their associated costs.
Prepare a list of all projects that may be desired or needed.	• A project that is deemed important to the operation may be omitted.	• List a full description of each project and its detailed costs by line item, and total the costs of all the projects.
Prepare the funding amounts to be spent on projects.	• Time may be wasted on reviewing projects that the operation cannot afford.	• Prepare amounts for contracted FF&E reserves and the owners' contracted or desired contributions for projects, based on the results of the annual forecast.
Prioritize the project listing by importance to the ongoing operation and the objectives of management.	• Monies available may be allocated to projects that are a lower priority.	• Using a plan agreed to by management, list the projects in priority order until the available budget is consumed. Maintain reserve amounts either by project or by total to plan for overcost situations.

Internal Control
A Fraud-Prevention Handbook for Hotel and Restaurant Managers

ISBN 0-937056-06-5; 10 chapters; ©1991 Hardbound

Author:
A. Neal Geller, Professor, Cornell University School of Hotel Administration

Internal control involves all the procedures you can implement and the forms you can use to document your transactions and make employee theft virtually impossible. Using everyday language, Professor Neal Geller tells you how actual operations use internal control to prevent fraud. You'll learn step-by-step procedures for controlling revenue from rooms, food and beverage outlets, and banquets.

The book explains how to:

- Divide duties, even in small shops
- Deal with cash transactions
- Prevent fraud in purchasing

Chapters contain *case studies* that demonstrate key points, *glossaries* that explain important terms, and *references* for further study.

Contents:
Foundations of Control; Cash Receipts; Accounts Receivable and Credit-Policy Issues; Purchasing and Expense Control; Payroll; Rooms-Income Control; Food & Beverage Control; Banquets and Conferences; Internal Control with Electronic Data Processing; An Overview of Internal Control.

Internal Control: A Fraud-Prevention Handbook for Hotel and Restaurant Managers is available only through The Cornell Campus Store.

For price and ordering information:
telephone, 607-255-5121
facsimile, 607-254-8075
e-mail, csbooks@cornell.edu

98-00245